THE COURT OF KING ROLF

THE COURT OF KING ROLF

Edited by Mark Walker

PARTRIDGE

LONDON · NEW YORK · TORONTO · SYDNEY · AUCKLAND

TRANSWORLD PUBLISHERS
61–63 Uxbridge Road, London W5 5SA
A division of The Random House Group Ltd.

RANDOM HOUSE AUSTRALIA PTY LTD
20 Alfred Street, Milsons Point, Sydney
New South Wales 2061, Australia

RANDOM HOUSE NEW ZEALAND
18 Poland Road, Glenfield, Auckland 10, New Zealand

RANDOM HOUSE SOUTH AFRICA (PTY) LTD
Endulini, 5a Jubilee Road, Parktown 2193, South Africa

Published 2000 by Partridge
a division of Transworld Publishers

A catalogue record for this book is available from the British Library.
ISBN 185225 2863

Set in 11/14pt Granjon by Falcon Oast Graphic Art

Printed in Great Britain by
Mackays of Chatham PLC, Chatham, Kent

1 3 5 7 9 10 8 6 4 2

CONTENTS

Preface by Mark Walker   9
Foreword by Michael Parkinson   11

1   THE ROYAL FAMILY   17
    Bruce Harris, Rolf's elder brother, recalls their childhood in Western Australia.
    Rolf's wife Alwen remembers their wedding and life together, as does their best
    man Alex Hausmann, and Bindi their daughter tells of her childhood and Rolf
    the grandfather. Brother-in-law Hugh Hughes speaks fondly of Rolf's parents,
    whilst nephew Buzz Hughes shares his varied memories.

2   FRIENDS, AUSTRALIANS AND COUNTRYMEN   40
    Fellow Australians the Honourable Bob Hawke AC, Barry Humphries, Clive
    James, Tim Farris, Ted Egan and Dennis Murphy air their thoughts on one of
    their country's favourite sons.

3   PORTRAIT PAINTERS   52
    Tony Hart speaks on the art of being Rolf. John Bellany remembers drawing on
    Rolf's many kindnesses, whilst Peter Murphy retraces *Rolf's Cartoon Club*. Mac,
    the *Daily Mail* cartoonist, brushes up on his technique and Zoë Jelley pictures
    the perfect holiday.

4   MINSTRELS IN THE GALLERY   66
    Laurie Holloway recalls making music with Rolf in the Sixties, Barry Booth
    takes us around Rolf's world, while DJ Simon Bates recounts the story of Rolf's
    musical rebirth in the early Nineties. Bob Clifford talks about putting the band
    together; Bernard O'Neill, Graeme Taylor, Mick Gaffey, Alan Dunn and Rick
    Bolton give us an insight into life on the road with Rolf and, finally, Michael

Eavis, the festival organizer, describes Rolf's triumphant appearance at Glastonbury in 1993.

5 INSTRUMENTS OF TORTURE   88
The story of the Stylophone is transmitted by Burt Coleman, Dana Gillespie vocalizes her thoughts on Rolf's verbal musicianship, Shining Bear blows his didgeridoo and Kate and Paddy Bush define Rolf's contribution to world music.

6 PHYSICIANS AND BEASTS   100
BBC Director of Programmes, Lorraine Heggessey, leads members of the *Animal Hospital* team with her memories of the show's origin. The team includes series producer Tina Bailey and co-presenter Rhodri Williams, the vets David Grant and Tessa Bailey, along with Noel and Trudy Jones, owners of a cat named Tom!

7 WONDROUS CREATURES   116
Special guests Joanna Lumley, John Cleese and Michaela Strachan recall their appearances on *Rolf's Amazing World Of Animals*, whilst Dale Templar, producer of the programme, remembers some of her favourite off-camera moments from the show.

8 HISTORICAL FIGURES   125
Long before Rolf was cartoon-timing or hospitalizing animals he was hosting his own shows. They are remembered here by producer Stewart Morris, choreographer Dougie Squires and actor George Claydon.

9 COURT JESTERS   133
The role call of pantomime colleagues includes producer Paul Elliott, Lorraine Chase, Gary Wilmot, Bonnie Langford, Carmen Silvera and June Whitfield. Oh yes it does!

10 ADVISERS AND EQUERRIES   145
Syd Gillingham, Rolf's press agent from 1962–94, remembers promotion, Phil Dale recalls his apprenticeship, while current English manager Jan Kennedy and her PA Lisa Ratcliff reflect on Rolf's boundless energy. Pat Lake-Smith, Rolf's current press agent, markets her man.

11 ROYAL BOUNTY   155
Sir Cliff Richard, the first president of Phab, and John Corless talk of Rolf's
charity work, and Barbara Bate, organizer of the Young Pavement Artist of the
Year Award, describes a day in the life of Rolf at a charity event.

12 SUBJECTS AND COURTIERS   161
Led by the president of the Rolf Harris Fan Club, Tony Cordwell, members
speak of their high regard for King Rolf. Devotees include the Morgan family,
Chris Woodall and Adele Broderick.

13 PEERS OF THE REALM   170
Friends and colleagues from the world of show business offer their counsel: Val
Doonican shares times with Rolf's parents, Chris Tarrant finds there's no escape
and Roger Whittaker sings Rolf's praises. Matthew Kelly talks facial hair, while
Barbara Windsor recalls a gallant Robin Hood and *Blue Peter* presenter Stuart
Miles looks on in awe.

14 KNIGHTS OF THE ROUND TABLE   184
Please be upstanding for Sir Harry Secombe and Sir George Martin.

15 THE KING'S SPEECH   190
King Rolf denies all the charges laid before him.

Lyrics   192

Preface by Mark Walker

Having played in Rolf's band for several years, I have seen at first hand the genuine love and warmth that abounds between Rolf, his peers, colleagues and audience. Within a month of my first performance with Rolf I had been alongside him backstage at the Shepherd's Bush Empire, where Robbie Williams seemed genuinely thrilled to be taking a lesson on the didgeridoo from Rolf, and also in front of over 40,000 screaming fans in Leeds, where Rolf turned on the city's Christmas lights. And that was just the beginning; I've had a fantastic time ever since. Consequently, it has been an honour and a joy to compile this book for Rolf's seventieth birthday.

When working closely with a star like Rolf it is easy to assume that you know almost everything about him. How mistaken could I be? The diversity of Rolf's life and career is so wide that it came as a considerable shock to find I knew only a fraction of the man. Early on in the book's creation, I spent a day at the Putney Animal Hospital. Watching the enormous amount of work and effort that goes into the programme from both Rolf and the team allowed me to see a side of Rolf that was completely alien and quite enlightening. Since then, I have interviewed and talked to so many different people who have spent time with Rolf in such a variety of situations that I have been completely astounded by the amount Rolf has accomplished in his life, both on and off the screen. 'What you see is what you get' may be a description that trips off the tongue of everyone who works with Rolf, but most of us don't know the half of it! To all the contributors and their agents, PAs and managers, I give my sincere thanks for their time and assistance.

I would like also to thank Adam Sisman, Shauna Newman and Sheila Lee, the team from Transworld, for their support and advice; my agent Tony Peake; Adam Hargreaves, Ben Goodger and Dave Burluck for their initial counsel; Tot Taylor for my original connection with Rolf; all the chaps in the band, including Hugh and Tony, for their support, encouragement and fun; the transcription team of Sue Lewis, Sally Walker (aka Mum!), Elaine McErlean, Paul Cooper and especially my PA Krysia McKillop, without whom I could never have completed the book in time. Very special thanks to my wife Claire and children Jessie, Joe and Madeleine, who put up with a present yet absent father in the house for the duration. And not least, thanks to the man himself, Rolf Harris, for his trust in allowing me to follow through my idea and giving me access to his extensive and bountiful records and archive material not to mention a heap of cartoons to help illustrate the book.

In recognition of this and all the contributors who gave their time and input free of charge, I will be donating some of my royalties from the book to Phab and the Joseph Patrick Memorial Trust for children with muscular dystrophy. My own contribution to this book is dedicated to the memory of my father, Paul Walker.

Foreword by Michael Parkinson

The public are not daft. They decided a long time ago that Rolf Harris was a good bloke, and they were right. But there is more to his continuing popularity than being a pleasant human being. There is the small matter of talent. Or, in his case, the large matter of talent.

Rolf Harris is one of those gifted individuals to whom difficult disciplines like singing, painting and acting the fool seem as natural as breathing.

Then there is the range of his appeal. He is a septuagenarian equally at home on a university campus in front of an audience of students as he is singing 'Nellie Dean' to people who remember the song from when it was a hit first time round.

I have known him thirty years or more. We are friends and next-door neighbours. His house is a clutter of paintings, his garden a riot of totem poles and bits of wood and tree root he has collected because he found something appealing about their shape and texture. It is the house and garden of an inquisitive, artistic man, and, I should add, family, because all of Rolf's nearest and dearest share his passions.

I have worked with Rolf in a professional capacity. He is the ideal talk-show guest in that he can talk the leg off an iron pot – an old Aussie expression – and also do a turn.

The interview I remember with most affection occurred in Sydney in the early Eighties. Rolf's dad had died shortly before and he was eager to show a video clip introducing his dad on stage at a concert. I was dubious. I know Rolf to be an emotional man and I wondered if he had done with grieving. He said he had, so we went ahead with his plan.

On the day of the recording the interview was going well; we were discussing his relationship with his late father and I introduced the clip. As soon as Rolf saw his father he started to cry; he was grief-stricken.

While the audience in the studio could see what was happening, the audience at home couldn't because they were watching the video clip.

In such a situation the host is faced with a dilemma. It is tempting and easy to exploit grief and imagine the headlines in the next day's newspaper. It is more of a problem to try to contain the situation so the sentiment is expressed without becoming mawkish and sentimental.

As we were approaching the end of the clip, with Rolf in tears, I suddenly remembered that he had told me his father was a funny man who loved a joke. So, in desperation, I said, 'You told me your dad laughed a lot. What sort of things appealed to his sense of humour?' It worked. Rolf told a funny story about his dad and it was like a cloud clearing the sun.

It illustrates that emotion is never far from the surface with Rolf Harris. You can see it when he does *Animal Hospital*. He often treads an emotional tightrope and, more than anything, I think this vulnerability explains his public appeal.

His other great gift is that he wears his talent lightly. Whether he is painting, singing, playing an instrument, telling jokes or generally mucking around, he manages to create the illusion he is not performing, merely doing his party piece.

What I admire most about Rolf is his ability to be both a star and an ordinary bloke. It is best illustrated by the way he supports the local cricket club in the village where we live.

For nearly thirty years now we have organized an annual charity game between a showbiz XI and the local team. Moreover, the night before, we have a charity cabaret dinner, and every year, without fail, Rolf turns up to entertain both the diners and the crowd at the cricket match.

One year I didn't ask him to perform the cabaret; he had done it so often I felt he deserved a rest. When I explained my reasons he just laughed at the suggestion that he might take it easy and later turned up with his didgeridoo and did an hour. No problem.

One year we had the idea that Rolf might sit at a table near the pavilion and draw cartoons of children if their parents made a donation to charity. He started at about lunchtime and you couldn't see him for children.

Long after the game was over, I was back at home, feet up, vowing never to do it again, when there was a knock at my door. It was about ten o'clock in the evening, and I wondered who on earth could be bothering me at such a late hour. Grouchily, I opened the door and there was Rolf. He had banknotes in his hatband, stuck in his belt and protruding from every orifice. He also had two plastic bags full of money.

'Just finished,' he said. 'Thought I'd bring you the proceeds.' Long after we had all departed, he had stayed behind until every last patron was satisfied. He'd finished his cartoons by lamplight. But the most amazing part of the whole business was that Rolf didn't think it was amazing.

So you can see why I like him as a bloke and admire him as a human being. It is reassuring that there are people like Rolf Harris running around this planet of ours. It gives you hope for the future, particularly when you consider his greatest achievement is that he has reached the age of seventy without ever growing old.

THE COURT OF KING ROLF

1

THE ROYAL FAMILY

Since stepping into the spotlight over forty years ago, Rolf has lived his public life in the glare of the world's media. He has always enjoyed the attention and acclaim that celebrity brings, but has also relished the private moments alone at home with his family. Anyone who knows Rolf Harris understands how important his family is to him. Quite apart from the love and affection they share, Rolf's parents, who are sadly no longer alive, his wife Alwen and daughter Bindi, along with his brother Bruce and Alwen's brother Hugh, have helped keep Rolf's feet firmly on the ground – and his chin up – throughout his career. Rolf is renowned for the joy he brings to his colleagues and audience, but that joy springs from the backbone that is his family.

It seems fitting that we should start our journey round the Court of King Rolf by hearing first from the people who are closest to him, starting with the only man alive who has known Rolf since the day he was born, his elder brother Bruce.

BRUCE HARRIS

Bruce Harris is a highly successful businessman who made his fortune in one of Australia's largest advertising firms. Six years older than Rolf, he is blessed with the same incredible energy. He is still heavily involved in various projects, including looking after Rolf's career worldwide and working out basic policies and directions for Rolf behind the scenes. Here he recalls their childhood together in Perth, Western Australia.

In Western Australia, he's called 'The Boy from Bassendean'.

How do you start to describe your kid brother? He is six years younger than I am, and I never fail to be knocked out by his talents.

I don't recall much about him as an infant, but he started to impinge on my consciousness when he was a toddler. By then we had moved from one side of Perth to the other. First we lived quite close to City Beach, near the Indian Ocean, which is about as far west as you can go in Australia, but after Rolf was born my father Crom, short for Cromwell, and mother Marge, short for Agnes Margaret, scouted around and found two adjoining blocks of land with river frontage. The river was the Swan, which trickles down from the Darling Ranges and swells as it flows through river flats, opening out to wash the feet of the lovely capital city of Perth before romping down to meet the sea near the port of Fremantle.

In those days, the early Thirties, the suburb they chose, Bassendean, seemed a long way from the city; it was all of seven miles! Back then it was like living in the country. Dad built our house himself. While it was being built we lived in a rented place not far away. Once we moved in, it was great; we had a kind of Huckleberry Finn existence. There were lots of trees to climb along the riverbank and a calm river to swim or fish in – and even nearly drown in. Rolf must have been a little over three years of age when one day he vanished. When he turned up to our frantic mother half an hour later he was dripping wet. It turned out he'd gone along the riverbank to the jetty Dad had built and fallen in. Somehow he'd managed to paddle back to the bank. That's when our parents decided Rolf must be taught to swim. In six months' time he was like a small white dolphin in the water. He could swim above it and under it. His brush with fate hadn't made him afraid of the water, it simply became a challenge to overcome. And this is an enduring positive trait of Rolf's.

It wasn't long after he had learned to swim that he met an even more life-threatening challenge, and one that snatched him away from the family for nearly six months: he contracted scarlet fever. In those days there were no miracle drugs and no antibiotics. Scarlet fever was a frightening, highly infectious and often fatal disease. Rolf, at about the age of four, was whisked into an infectious-diseases hospital and quarantined from the family for months. None of us, parents included, was permitted to see him. When he was allowed out, Marge was horrified. Rolf had been allowed to run around in the hospital too early after spending over a month in bed and his ankles and legs were bowed. Even worse, he had been the only child on a ward of adults and, as a result, his language wasn't too pretty. Marge, still fresh from England, was mortified. She had always taught and encouraged us to speak properly, with rounded vowels and crisp, clear endings to sentences. She took Rolf to a paediatrician to see what could be done about his legs, and they twisted them back into shape and encased them in plaster. Consequently, some of my memories of Rolf as a child are of watching and hearing him clumping about the house, looking like a tiny skiing-accident victim! He was in those plaster legs for over a year to correct his ankles and posture. Unlike his legs, Mother believed she was never able to correct his new accent, though she tried with elocution lessons and frequent corrections when he spoke.

Later, when I was supposed to be learning to play the piano accordion, I didn't practise, so Rolf took it over. He also showed an interest in the piano and was sent to learn to play at a local convent, where a sister took him in hand, literally. She was a stickler for tempo; Rolf had to be perfectly in time with the beat and count out loud as he played. When he didn't play to the correct tempo, she would hammer it out on his hands with a wooden ruler. She taught him well. He'll tell you now that there's always a metronome beating in his brain whenever he's playing or singing.

As I entered my teens, Rolf became – in my eyes – more and more outrageous. I thought he was a complete show-off. He took to singing loudly in the street, doing cartwheels and making all kinds of weird noises. I would pretend I didn't know him. I was far more conservative than Rolf. It was at about that time that he began to show his artistic skills as well. We must have had a genetic ability. Our grandfather on Crom's side was a portrait painter in Wales in the days before photography took over. He was a Royal Academician. His brother – also a fine portrait artist – had travelled to India in the days of the Raj to paint portraits of maharajahs. Dad's brothers and sisters included three artists, two of them commercial artists, and one a book illustrator and author. Crom himself was quite an accomplished watercolourist. It therefore wasn't surprising that Rolf began to demonstrate a talent for drawing and painting.

During the Second World War I ended up in the army and after training I was sent off to Darwin, where I lost close touch with Rolf for some years. Meanwhile he was in high school. He sat for, and won, a scholarship to Modern School, a prestigious Perth secondary school for bright children and, as I had before him, he became an excellent competitive swimmer, first with the Perth Swimming Club, where he demonstrated considerable prowess, and later with the Bassendean club, which he helped to start. I remember him telling me that, as a lowly first year at Perth Modern School, he entered every event in the swimming carnival – freestyle, breaststroke and backstroke – in all age groups. The sports master reprimanded him for being so arrogant, but Rolf won all the events he'd entered, becoming something of a school hero.

While still at Modern School, and encouraged by the former national backstroke champion Percy Oliver, Rolf decided to enter the Australian National Swimming Championships, which were to be held in Melbourne. Rolf was told he could compete, but he'd have to find his own airfare. To help raise the funds Rolf, supported by the people of Bassendean, put on a fund-raising performance in the interval at the Saturday night pictures. He could now play piano quite well, and was working on his own versions of various comic songs he'd heard on the radio, including one called 'Seven Beers with the Wrong Woman', and somehow he managed to put on a half-hour performance.

To cut a long story short, the collection donated by those ordinary movie goers of Bassendean provided the money to enable him to catch the plane with the rest of the team. Percy Oliver had given Rolf the treasured silk swimming costume he had worn at the 1936 Berlin Olympics, and Rolf swears that wearing it helped him win his race in Melbourne. He came back to Perth as Australian junior backstroke champion.

It wasn't long afterwards that Rolf entered the long-running, top-rating national radio show *Australia's Amateur Hour* and, with his outrageous version of 'Seven Beers with the Wrong Woman', won the most votes for his performance. That led to him being offered a slot in a stage variety show at Her Majesty's Theatre in Perth.

And the rest, as they say in the classics, is history!

ALWEN HARRIS

In 1952 Rolf travelled to London to attend art college, where he first met his future Welsh wife, Alwen Hughes. A successful artist and sculptress in her own right, Alwen has been married to Rolf for over forty years. The couple have one daughter, Bindi, and a grandson, Marlon. There are very few marriages that endure the strains and pressures that celebrity brings, but Rolf and Alwen have a powerful bond that springs from their shared enthusiasm for life. With Rolf it was pretty much love at first sight, but it took Alwen a while longer to fall for her Antipodean Romeo . . .

I met Rolf when we were at art school, at the City & Guilds in Kennington, and at first I didn't like him at all! He was always acting the fool, leering around his easel and embarrassing me. I thought he was an absolute show-off, so I went out with everyone who asked me except him. I think that put his back up. I progressed to the Royal College, and didn't see him again until I was exhibiting at the Royal Academy, where he happened to be exhibiting at the same time. When Rolf saw me, in his enthusiasm he picked me up and carried me across the room. I wasn't too pleased at that either! Anyway, we exchanged telephone numbers and went our separate ways.

Apparently Rolf tried phoning many times when I was out, but in those days there were no answer phones, so I was unaware that he'd rung. It was quite a time before he got through to me and, when he did, I agreed to go for dinner with some of his friends. That was our first real get together, in 1956. We went to a Lyons Corner House called the Grill and Cheese at Marble Arch. We had a super meal, and afterwards, as we walked down Oxford Street, he said, 'Aren't you nice?' I stopped, looked him straight in the eye and said, 'Yes I am!' He nearly died!

We got married in 1958. I had a studio opposite the church at Maida Vale, so I walked across to the service, taking my poodle Pugsy as bridesmaid. We had a very small wedding, with my mum and dad and a few friends, and a party afterwards in my studio. I remember Rolf losing his car; he had been determined that no-one would put silly things all over it, and promptly forgot where he'd parked it. I think we were both working like mad at the time, so we never had a honeymoon.

lots of love
Alwen & Rolf

We lived in a flat by London Zoo, where I spent a lot of time studying. We could hear all the animals at night; it was lovely, with the lions roaring and the wolves howling. Pugsy lived there with us and we used to take her for walks on Primrose Hill.

It was through me that Rolf was introduced to animals. He didn't take a lot of notice of them until he met Pugsy. He couldn't believe that she didn't seem to like him and would have nothing to do with him. In fact, she used to come into the room, look at Rolf and turn her back. No matter what Rolf said to her she wouldn't look at him. To cure the problem, I shut Rolf and the dog in a room together with some balloons. I told Rolf to blow up the balloons and make funny squeaking noises with them, or let them go so they whooshed round the room, which was something Pugsy adored. Rolf was a bit reticent, but he did it and, from that day on, she accepted him.

I also taught Rolf to listen to silence; he'd never heard it before. I took him up onto Dartmoor, and he was whistling and carrying on as usual – even in those days he could never keep quiet! I said, 'For goodness' sake, shut up and listen!' He was amazed by the wonder of the silence. It seemed to stun him rigid. As a child I roamed the Fells up in the Lakes and North Wales. My grandfather taught me how to listen to silence, and I loved it. So initially it was hard for me to deal with the fact that Rolf was so noisy.

At that time Rolf was doing a bit on children's television and performing regularly at the Down Under Club in Earl's Court. That was when he first performed 'Tie Me Kangaroo Down, Sport', which he wrote in the Grill and Cheese. We went there quite regularly for lunch, and one day he wrote most of the verses on the back of a menu while we were eating. He sang it to my father, but being a typical major from the army, he was a little disgusted by it. 'Load of rubbish!' he said.

In 1964 Bindi was born. From the moment she could hold a pen Bindi was drawing. She did some absolutely fabulous pictures as a child. Rolf and I never really taught her. You can't teach a naturally talented person, you simply supply the materials. We were in the doctor's surgery one day, and to keep her amused the doctor said,

'Draw me an elephant!' He was amazed to see her not only draw an elephant, but draw it upside down so it would appear the right way up to him on the other side of the table. Whenever we travelled, which was a great deal, I always gave her paper and felt pens. From a very early age Bindi would do portraits of people and get a likeness.

I sometimes wish Rolf would return to his painting, he could have yet another good career in that area. Rolf doesn't actually have to entertain at all, but he doesn't get any praise when he's painting alone, and as he is addicted to applause, that would be hard for him to give up. Rolf has had continuous praise all his life and has become accustomed to it. Sadly, he's very out of practice with his art now, and painting is one of those things that is hard to get back into. He can still do his huge paintings with a great big brush and emulsion paint, and his cartoons always come easily to him, but to do a landscape or a portrait is another matter.

I enjoy watching Rolf perform, as long as I'm not at the front of the audience. I have always particularly enjoyed the times when things haven't gone according to plan. In 1963 Rolf had his only hit in the States with 'Tie Me Kangaroo Down, Sport' which got to number 5. Rolf was playing in Chicago, and on the opening night he leaned on his wobble-board and it slipped through a narrow gap in the stage. Rolf hit the floor and was stranded. It was his opening number and he had thrown his instrument away! They sent someone down to the

bowels of the theatre to retrieve it but, as Rolf said afterwards, it felt like it took them about eight hours to return with the thing! Another time he split his trousers up the back and had to wear one of the band's sweaters tied round his waist to hide it. Things like that make me die with laughter.

Being with Rolf all these years has been wonderful, but there is obviously a negative aspect to Rolf's fame. Bindi missed out on a lot in her childhood. He couldn't take her to the zoo, or do similar things that a father would normally do, without being mobbed. Rolf's always been upset about that. He was also often away at important times, like when she broke her wrist, or when she came down with mumps. I'm sure there are many famous dads who have had the same problems, because the public will never let you be normal. They don't mean anything by recognizing him and wanting to talk to him, but they don't realize how that can interfere with you just being a person at the same time. So, for example, you can only go to the zoo when it's closed and you've got special permission. That applies to a lot of things and is, in a way, the downside to fame. I don't mind being stared at or having cameras face us or anything like that, that doesn't worry me in the slightest, but when you really want to do something together and aren't allowed to, that is a little sad.

It's never been a quiet life with Rolf, but it's been great fun, and I love him to bits. He has always worked so hard, but he does occasionally relax. He whittles away at a piece of wood or polishes a bit of stone. It can drive me mad! There's continuous sanding. He even did it on a journey out to Australia, until someone on the plane came up to him and said, 'Would you mind stopping that infernal racket?' He

gets carried away, but that's the only way he relaxes. It's like practising a musical instrument: it's fine if you are the one doing it, but it can be absolutely horrifying for those around you. As was the case when Rolf was learning the didgeridoo. Rolf has always made weird noises, but that was horrendous. He got it in the end, thankfully, and he's been blowing his own didgeridoo ever since!

ALEX HAUSMANN

Alex Hausmann is one of Rolf's oldest friends, and was best man at Rolf and Alwen's wedding in March 1958. Born in Stuttgart, Alex, like Rolf, was an expat living in London in the early Fifties.

When I was first in England I lodged in a boarding house in Earls Court Square, London. One morning I was making my way downstairs for breakfast, happily minding my own business, when suddenly a gentleman came out of a room with nothing on but a pair of trousers. He looked at me and said, 'Hi, how are you?' It was a typically English boarding house, and no-one had spoken to me there before, so I was pleasantly surprised and stayed to talk to him for a while. He explained to me that he came from Australia and asked where I came from, and we arranged to meet up later that day. At the time I was in a hurry because I had to have breakfast and go straight to my office. We had hardly sat down in the breakfast room, when the self-same gentleman, barefoot and still only wearing a pair of trousers, came in and looked at everyone. 'Come on,' he said, 'give us a big smile, you lot!' All the old dears virtually dropped their spoons and stared at him with their mouths wide open. That was my first close encounter with Rolf.

Over the following month we became very good friends and shared many meals together, including cold ones in our rooms. Sometimes we would come home and there would be a note on the desk when we came in saying, 'No dinner tonight. Three shillings being deducted from your rent,' because the landlady was too lazy to cook. We got to know each other well, and at the same time Rolf helped me to improve my English.

This was quite a long time before Rolf met Alwen, and in those days we had plenty of female company. There was a nurses' residence opposite where we lived in Earls Court, and the girls used to mend our socks while Rolf played the squeezebox for them. Rolf started to earn a little money playing the squeezebox at the Down Under Club. His savings had run out and he had to earn some cash to pay the rent in the boarding house, which in those days was three guineas a week, so at that time Rolf did quite a lot of portrait paintings for families he got to know and played the squeezebox for about three pounds a week in the Down Under Club! I used to accompany him there, and whenever he played 'Waltzing Matilda' tears would roll down the girls' cheeks, so we had to look after them attentively, which we didn't mind.

When Alwen came along, I felt that she and Rolf worked well together as a couple compared with other girlfriends he'd had. Alwen was always jolly and a good laugh, but her work as an artist and sculptress was something new to me; coming from the financial and business world, it was something I hadn't been acquainted with and had to learn to understand.

By that time I had become very close to Rolf. In a way we were growing up together in England, like brothers. He would come over to Germany with me at Christmas and other holidays, and had got to know my family well. He even started to speak a few words of German. My family thought Rolf was most amusing, though, of course, at the beginning I had to translate from English to German. But musical people are gifted at learning languages and expressing themselves and Rolf got on with everybody like a house on fire, often using the wrong words I had taught him in German – including swear words – to the great amusement of everyone. Rolf has never been a drinker and he wasn't used to drinking much alcohol. Once Rolf had a glass or two, and I saw him in the corner in the afternoon, fast asleep and snoring, with everyone sitting round him. He was most embarrassed.

You're only as old as you feel (that's a shock!)

I was very honoured to be asked by Rolf to be his best man when he and Alwen got married. The wedding was in Maida Vale, and Rolf wanted to have wedding rings for both of them. In those days, in England it was very unusual for the groom to have a wedding ring. But they had bought two rings in Spain on holiday. In the church, I had the rings in my pocket and, as best man, I was also looking after the bridesmaid. Well, holding on to the bridesmaid, who happened to be Alwen's poodle! Alwen had obtained special permission to bring the dog into the church for the ceremony. When the minister asked the customary question about whether anyone knew of any lawful reason why the couple shouldn't be wed, apparently I cleared my throat. I handed over the rings to the minister to give to the couple, and on the way down the aisle, Rolf turned round and whispered, 'You bastard, I thought you were going to say something!'

The reception was held at Alwen's studio, and they had a very unusual wedding cake, which was exactly a yard long, without any tiers. There were a lot of amusing people at the party, which went on for hours, until Rolf and Alwen went off to see *Around the World in Eighty Days*.

At that time Rolf was just beginning to work on television. He performed with his puppet Willoughby, which I think gave him his first break on TV, and over the next few years he became more and more successful. I was very proud to have him as a friend, but what I appreciated most about Rolf was that he didn't let it go to his head. He stayed as normal as ever.

We have remained close friends over the years. I remember coming to London in 1971 for Rolf's first appearance on *This is Your Life*, as well as his second one in 1995. For the first one, with Eamonn Andrews, Rolf's parents were still alive, and his father came over from Australia, flying for the first time in his life. Before I came on they started playing 'Two Little Boys', and when it came to the bit where Eamonn said, 'And then you went to England, to Earls Court . . .' before he could finish Rolf interrupted with '. . . and then met Alex!'

I told the story of our parting one night after an Australian party we had been to at Beaufort Gardens. We came home to the boarding house afterwards and were talking about what we were doing the next day. I meant to say 'How shall we leave it?' but doing a quick literal translation from German in my head it came out, 'How shall we remain?'

Rolf stuck his hand out and said, 'Friends, I hope!'

'How shall we remain?' has been our standard greeting ever since.

BINDI HARRIS

Bindi Harris is Rolf and Alwen's daughter. They named her after the town Bindi Bindi in Western Australia, a place noted for its beautiful Bindi stones. Being the daughter of a major celebrity undoubtedly has its draw-backs, but Bindi is immensely proud of her father. Like her mother, Alwen, Bindi is a successful artist in her own right. Bindi has a son, Marlon, who dotes on his grandfather.

Cartoon by a young Bindi

Dad will often place a big piece of paper on the floor and draw something with Marlon using large felt tips. He used to do that with me when I was young. We would draw on paper tablecloths in restaurants, starting with a scribble and then turning it into something. As a child I used to spend most of my time drawing, and it was encouraging to see my pictures framed and hung up on the wall; it made me feel very special. Art has always been something I do and it would have been strange if I hadn't become an artist. Mum is a sculptress and jeweller, Dad does painting and drawing, Auntie Pixie 'O' Harris was a children's illustrator, Rolf's dad made lovely paintings in private and my great-great-grandfather, George F. Harris, was a portrait painter in Wales.

Dad and I have a totally different way of seeing things in paint. Dad has a method of painting tonally, which he loves to do in a very impressionistic way, and he is so clever at getting a likeness with caricatures and portraits. It has been a slight bone of contention that I can't really get the tonal thing, though I have tried. My way of painting is just different from his, and recently I was very touched when he asked me if I could teach him to paint from his emotions and imagination, as I do. I paint rather large, colourful, symbolic paintings, and I think I learned to dare to be big and bold from watching my dad paint his large Aussie landscapes on stage. I think Dad would dearly love to take my hand and make it paint as he sees it, as neither of us understands what the other does, and yet we are both valid and secretly we each think the other is great!

Mum and Dad never pushed me with art, but it was always assumed that I would be an artist. Art, photography and sculpture have been part of my family for generations. Conversations at home used to revolve around, 'When you go to art college, Bindi.' In fact, I did go to art college, but I left fairly early on in the course. I think I had to find out whether I had a passion for art, whether I was an artist, or whether that was simply what other people perceived me to be.

After a few years totally without art, working in fashion and record shops, I grew so depressed from missing painting that I gave up work and went back to portraiture, and then finally took my BA in Bristol. I've been painting ever since. I have always had my parents' support when it comes to my artwork, which I feel very lucky about.

Holidays were probably my favourite times in childhood. I used to love swimming and snorkelling with Dad. In Malta we used to do a lot of snorkelling, looking at the fish and coral, exploring in the water. Five years ago we visited the Grand Canyon and went to a Native American powwow. It wasn't a tourist show, it was a genuine pow-wow with about 200 Native Americans and twenty white people. We happened to come across it by chance.

No-one knows who Rolf Harris is in America, so he gets complete peace there. He grows his beard long, and it's great to see him relax. I noticed him doing some drawings, and suddenly he had a crowd of children round him. They didn't know who he was, but he has a gift for sharing a part of himself with people and basically entertaining them. It's something inbuilt; people are magnetically drawn to my father. I don't know what it is, and I don't think he knows, either, but it is a gift.

Dad is a very funny man, but he doesn't know how truly comical he is in everyday life, without the jokes, just as himself. Especially when he gets annoyed, then he's very entertaining. Putting his foot in it and not reading the subtleties of a situation are his specialities. If someone has a wooden leg he'll tell a wooden-leg joke and not notice any of our hints until it's too late. He never means any harm and it's all incredibly innocent. He is always enthusiastic about life – sometimes a little blindly, but it's an endearing quality.

Dad will tell you what a perfect childhood he had; it was very free and he was always encouraged by his parents. I have wonderful memories of my grandfather on my father's side, Crom; he was a tall, silent man with a tangible gentleness. He didn't follow a religion as far as I'm aware, but he was the most Christian man I have ever met. He would do anything for anyone; he would give the food from his plate to anyone who needed it. He had a beautiful heart and was very hard-working. Marge, my grandmother, was a force to be reckoned with; she was stubborn and forceful and made Dad practise his piano, but without her he probably wouldn't be able to play music with the freedom and joy he does today. I know he misses them both so much. Crom especially. He was a silent pillar of strength, and was always there for Dad to run to and show what he'd been up to that day. Even though they have both passed away, I feel as if Dad still looks for their approval and that that is what keeps him going. He also wants to encourage others to be the best they can be, as he knows how lucky he was to be supported by his parents to follow his own talents.

HUGH HUGHES

Hugh Hughes is Alwen Harris's younger brother. Brought up in England, he emigrated to Australia in 1967, where he visited the home of Rolf's parents, Marge and Crom, in Bassendean, Perth. Since his return to England Hugh has taken on the role of Rolf's stage manager, accompanying Rolf on most of his appearances.

I had just left school and was still very wet behind the ears when this guy came down to Devon with my sister for the weekend. In those days our parents ran a small hotel and it was fully booked. I remember being hauled out onto the lawn with a tent. There wasn't a room for my sister's companion, either, so he was hauled out, too, and we spent the night together. Hence I can lay claim to having slept with Rolf Harris in his early days, for my sister's companion was none other than he!

I remember being very impressed by Rolf, though at that time, to me, he was simply Alwen's date. He seemed an especially relaxed, cool sort of fellow, and I liked him from the word go. I don't know what impression he made with my parents, though they let him marry their daughter. Not that they could have stopped the marriage, even if they'd wanted to. Their wedding was quite an eye-opener for me. When Alwen was a student in London I would occasionally visit her, and we would partake in the usual student pastimes: going out, sharing a glass of beer and having fun. Then, it seemed almost out of the blue, I was attending Rolf and Alwen's wedding. The press was all over them like a rash, and it was a completely alien world for me.

One of the best things about the service was that Alwen had her lovely poodle, Pugsy, with her during the marriage ceremony. Next day the papers caught on to this and the headlines were MARRY ME, MARRY MY DOG! I sometimes wish people could accept that there is a connection between other living creatures and ourselves. To me, this is the reason Rolf's work with animals is so significant: it helps to open up people's hearts.

This brings me briefly to Rolf's spiritual side. I don't think he was ever very religious, but he certainly started on what is called 'the spiritual path' a few years ago, and it has had a wonderful effect on his life and outlook. The real catalyst for this occurred in the presence of the great Sai Baba in India. Sai Baba is considered by hundreds of millions of people from a cross section of religions around the world to be the greatest spiritual leader alive today. I don't know whether Rolf has ever cried as he did then, either before or since. It's a very private thing for him, so I won't elaborate, but Rolf now appreciates that there is another existence beyond our earthly senses, and that better world can be reached, not through our mind, but through our hearts. When you see Rolf on TV or on stage, he openly communicates from his heart.

From Alwen and Rolf's wedding, the gift they received from Rolf's parents is the thing that most stands out in my memory. Marge and Crom lived in Australia and couldn't be present, but they sent over a large box of Australian wild flowers, bush, banksia and nuts. I'd never seen anything like it, and it was very touching for Rolf because he was so close to his parents. I knew he missed his home and the bush, and seeing all these wild flowers gave me a better appreciation of the different country and culture he had come from.

Rolf was very close to his parents, and their passing caused him a great deal of heartache. They gave Rolf and his brother Bruce a wonderful childhood; it was very wild and free. I visited their house in Bassendean, which is a suburb of Perth on the River Swan. They lived on the banks of the river, surrounded by trees and quite secluded from the outside world. Rolf and Bruce had a lot of freedom, and I think Rolf probably misses that. He often talks about playing in the river and climbing the trees barefoot in just a pair of shorts. Rolf has always been grateful to his parents for giving him the freedom to learn through experience.

Marge and Crom actually built the house at Bassendean. Rolf's father was a very quiet man. He wasn't given to expressing his emotions, whether they were joy or rage. He would always walk away from trouble rather than get involved, and Rolf is much the same. Marge actually ran the show; theirs was a maternal home. She was a highly intelligent lady; I think she was one of the first women in Wales to get a degree in mathematics. She was very much into the Rolf Harris legend. As a stranger, within five seconds of meeting her you would know she was Rolf Harris's mum. She was incredibly proud of both her sons, because, of course, Bruce is a hugely successful businessman. What Rolf has achieved in entertainment Bruce has achieved in business. Though she never basked in their success for her own glory, it was simply that these were her sons who had made good. In contrast, with Crom you would probably never know who his sons were; he was the quiet one, but he was no less very proud of them.

One of the major differences between Australia and England is that Australians tend to nurture a go-for-it disposition, whereas the English are far more reserved and reticent. Rolf actually got into television because nobody told him that he couldn't. He wanted to do it, so he did! Of course, at that time it was the birth of light entertainment on television, so there were no rules. For instance, in the days of his variety shows, the established norm was for a line of dancing girls, such as the 'TV Tappers', to high kick their way across the stage. For Rolf's shows a gaggle of teenagers dressed in the lastest Carnaby Street gear would dance their own thing in an organized fashion. It was free expression and it was like a breath of fresh air. Also, the camera techniques were groundbreaking in that the main subject didn't always hog centre picture but might be seen in the corner or side of the shot.

As Rolf became more famous during the Sixties I didn't perceive any change in him as a person. There were expectations for him to behave in a certain way and pursue a lavish and ostentatious lifestyle, as many stars did, but Rolf stayed the same. He even carried on driving around in his Morris Traveller! Which was fortunate, as I hate to think of the damage he could have done behind the steering wheel of a powerful sports car, because although he won't believe this, Rolf is not the world's greatest driver. Even now Rolf lives relatively simply. He's addicted to the applause and celebrity, but he's definitely

not addicted to the fortune, because he has never lived a flashy lifestyle.

He's also addicted to the work. Over the years, Rolf became more of a workaholic and spent more and more time on some planet in a distant galaxy far away! But then, where else does one invent a man with three legs who sings his life story? You can imagine the scene at his home the night before the show. Alwen and our mother were attempting to sew the Jake the Peg costume by hand with hopelessly inadequate instructions from Rolf, who could see the finished product in his mind's eye, but was in too high a state of nerves and fully wound up. How it ever came to fruition I'll never know, but that's showbiz!

I have a snapshot in my mind of Rolf in Devon. We found a beautiful beech tree that had been blown over and, having got permission from the farmer whose land it was on, we were cutting off some of its branches. Rolf and I both love to work with wood, but we have strong views about conservation, so we only use wood from trees that have fallen. Rolf had been working away for a while when I called him. He shot up from the leaves and undergrowth with the most wondrous expression on his face, as if he was completely at home. Those are the times when Rolf is in his element.

BUZZ HUGHES

Buzz Hughes is Rolf's nephew. A successful jeweller by trade, Buzz has recently been staying with Rolf and Alwen, helping Rolf to learn to use his computer, and on occasions driving him to work – though not if he can avoid it!

My earliest memories of Uncle Rolf are of him coming to my school. My parents had emigrated from England to a small country town in Australia, and when he visited once they stopped lessons for the day. He played his instruments, sang songs and did a painting for the school. It was magnificent and made me feel incredibly special, but although I remember that occasion, his being a personality never really occurred to me in childhood. Obviously I saw him on television, but to me he was just a man doing strange things on TV; I didn't equate that with the person I saw at my house, carving wood and polishing stones. It didn't occur to me that my uncle was a celebrity until a friend and I took him down to the market near home and had to dress him up in a hat and dark glasses.

The times Rolf came to our house when I was a child were the times he could relax. He didn't have to perform there, although he is a naturally amusing, high-energy person; he can divert those energies to doing the things he loves just as easily as to an audience. Our place was a showbiz-free zone, and because we had an idyllic setting, it was a place he could escape the constraints of his public life. I don't know if that was a specific issue for Rolf, but privacy is important to the family.

We had a waterfall near where we lived, in Terrania Creek in northern New South Wales. At the base of the waterfall was a big swimming hole, which was filled with freezing rain-forest water. It was very isolated up there, and one time Rolf stripped off completely naked and jumped in. Suddenly two walkers came by while he was standing on the rocks under the falling water. They looked at him strangely, as if to say, No, it couldn't be? But Rolf found it funny; he's not pretentious or stuck up and he realizes where he comes from. I think that's the Australian in him shining through!

Lately I've been teaching Rolf to use his computer, and it's strange, he has a huge willingness to learn but not much to pay attention! I'm not sure he understands the logic behind it; it's a tool he thinks of as being a lot more complicated than it is. He has mastered e-mail now, and is amazed by its capabilities. When he appeared on the TV show *The Big Breakfast* he mentioned his website, and subsequently had a huge number of album sales over the net that day. The power of that isn't lost on Rolf, especially considering his ties to mass communication.

Rolf has even used the computer for his art. He made a beautiful collage of autumn leaves. He scanned each one in and then pasted them together. The colours were wonderful. I don't know if he did it for anything in particular, but there's always a project in the works with Rolf. The two of us designed his recent album cover on the computer. He still draws things free hand – he enjoys the flow of ideas that a pen, paper and paint give him – but then he likes to tweak them on the computer. He's got a million and one brilliant ideas, but it's not easy to do everything exactly as he wants! One of the interesting points about artists is their single-minded vision. They see the outcome before it's done, so sometimes collaboration doesn't work so well.

Driving Rolf is an area where collaboration can be interesting. I've established that it really makes no difference what you do. With Rolf, you could be driving like God on a cushion of air and you'd still be doing something wrong! You're going too fast, you're going too slow, or you're going from too slow to too fast, or you're turning the wheel more than is necessary, or you're braking harder than necessary. And the ultimate irony is that Rolf is a shocking driver! He's hard and soft on the pedal; he's all over it, and the funniest thing is that he doesn't see it. I think he genuinely believes he is an excellent driver. He's not, he's an awful driver, and awful to drive. But if you lay down the law and say, 'I'm driving you. Like it and enjoy, or I'll get out and you can drive,' he backpedals and says, 'Oh, I didn't mean it.' Strangely, Rolf loves his driver, who drives like a mad, crazed clown, but with his family he's very particular.

I have great respect for what Rolf has achieved. At home in Australia I have seen lots of beneficial attention brought to Aboriginal issues by Rolf. Through his years of work with indigenous people, he has contributed to the public consciousness of Australia, though he steers clear of a political stance. He knows what he believes and thinks is right, and that's what governs his actions. I think his ability to convey how genuine a person he is to millions of people shines through, and that has helped Rolf continue his success for so long.

2

FRIENDS, AUSTRALIANS
AND COUNTRYMEN

Rolf travelled to the UK in 1952, partly, according to Alwen, to escape the clutches of an over-exuberant girlfriend! Rolf's own version of events is that the girl in question wasn't overly keen on his parents, and their feelings were mutual. When Rolf decided he agreed with his mum and dad, a hasty exit to foreign lands seemed as good an escape as any. It also gave him the chance to see if he could stand on his own two feet, away from the constant help of his loving parents. Plus, of course, he wanted to attend art school, so that he could follow in his grandfather's footsteps as a portrait painter.

Since then, although Rolf has made his home in Britain, Australia has never been far from his heart, and annual excursions home to Australia have enabled him to keep in touch with the native land he holds so dear. As one of the country's most famous sons and the first antipodean entertainer to become hugely successful on the world stage, Australia, too, has a place in its heart for Rolf. Here, some of the country's leading figures pay tribute to their fellow Aussie.

BOB HAWKE

The Honourable Robert James Lee Hawke AC was Prime Minister of Australia between 1983 and 1991. In 1995 he contributed this tribute as part of the second This is Your Life *programme to be devoted to Rolf Harris. The first was in 1971.*

'Hi Rolf, I'm sorry I can't be with you, but I'm stuck here in this beautiful city of Sydney, with which you're very well acquainted. We've got the Opera House out there and, of course, that has a fairly special meaning for you, because you gave the first-ever public performance there when it was opened in 1973. Of course, our paths crossed much earlier than that, at the great educational institution in Western Australia, the Perth Modern School. I started there in 1942 and you were a year behind me. It was a great school and had a number of personalities, but you, Rolf Harris, were one of the very significant figures because you had such a range of talents. You rose to the top internationally very quickly, you've received honours all around the world, not least in your own country of Australia, where you were recognized with the Order of Australia in 1989. Rolf, I congratulate you as a great ambassador for Australia. I wish you well, have a great night!'

DAME EDNA EVERIDGE

Dame Edna has secretly admired Rolf since their first meeting many aeons ago.

My little whiskery friend, Rolf, has done wonderfully well for himself, as we Australians tend to do. Not many stars of black-and-white television are still up there at the top today. Many are at the bottom, and below it. Poor darlings. However, when Rolf once came to me for advice and TLC, I told him that one day he would be at the top of the tree. Little did I know that he'd be at the top of the tree trying to save a ruptured squirrel. Incidentally, possums, I happen to know animals adore his work as much as we do.

Here is a lovely anecdote, the better for being true:

I was staying in an internationally acclaimed, award-winning hotel in Perth, Western Australia – Rolf's hometown. Again, he desperately needed my help, so I called room service and ordered some scrummy tea and cakes. While we were waiting – in those days Australian room service was not the miracle of speed that it is today – Rolf told me his life story, and I naturally pretended I hadn't heard it before.

'What about that lovely song "Two Little Boys"?' I asked, suppressing a rude yawn (I'd had a late night).

His eyes brightened behind his bushy beard and famous face furniture.

'Oh, that's a lovely long story!' he exclaimed. 'Let me tell it to you in full.'

To my alarm, Rolf withdrew a funny thing from within his 45 per cent crimplene, 38 per cent seersucker and 60 per cent viscose powder-blue safari suit. It was his famous wokka-board with lager-phone extension.

'Where's that wretched kiwi fruit and pineapple sponge?' I fretted crabbily.

Rolf moved his chair very close to mine and began singing 'Two Little Boys' to instrumental accompaniment. Halfway through his serenade, the door opened and a nervous Aboriginal maid, her eyes like saucers, entered with coffee and scrambled eggs for three, but Rolf didn't stop singing. I could hardly interrupt him in order to give room service the sharp edge of my tongue, but it was a lesson in patience and tolerance that has made me a good listener ever since.

Good luck, Rolf darling, and congratulations on whatever it is I'm meant to be congratulating me for. Oh, yes! Happy eightieth birthday, darling.

CLIVE JAMES

Humorist, television presenter, satirist and wit, Clive James is another of Australia's famous exports.

THE BACKSTROKE SWIMMER, ROLF HARRIS

When young he was a backstroke champion,
Even to fans a fact not widely known.
Backstrokers lie down, look up at the sun
And must get used to being on their own.

Backstrokers squint to ward off the bright sky
And at the most they see where they have been.
His future lay behind him, how he'd fly
One day to great fame on a little screen.

The beard, the felt tips and the wobble-board,
The task of tying down a kangaroo –
These things the children of the world adored.
Small injured animals admire him, too.

Kittens up trees, dogs trapped in microwaves
Are grateful for his friendly, nasal drawl;
Tots lower hamsters into tiny graves
Sure that his tender heart sustains them all.

He was, is still, the incarnation of
The Australian spirit, spry yet down to earth:
Raw energy that taught itself to love
The strange life in the vast land of its birth.

The world has learned from him, and I likewise.
For me, however, what he has to teach
Starts where the spine-basher screwed up his eyes:
The loose, long-footed kick, the easy reach —

Signs of true power, which lies in power to spare.
The strength behind all useful gentleness
Is gained by seeing that the past is there
And what comes next a man can only guess.

He stretched, he yawned, and woke up to world fame.
He grinned, and children by the million grew
To adulthood still smiling at his name,
His laugh lines hard-earned from the harsh but true

Sting of chlorine, the flame that bleached the blue.

TIM FARRIS

As a member of the hugely successful INXS, Tim Farris is among the most innovative and respected musicians of his generation. Tim first met Rolf on a trip to the UK when he was a young boy, a meeting that had an important effect on his future chosen career.

My personal experiences with Rolf stretch back to my childhood, as he was a close friend of my aunt, Jennifer Ryan. I remember, in 1964, when I was very young, my family sailed to England from Perth to meet my father's parents, who were English. While we were staying with them, Rolf rang my mother, because she was Jennifer's sister, and invited us all to *The Rolf Harris Show*.

The programme affected my life in quite a dramatic way. Cilla Black and the Beatles performed on the show, and I have vague memories of meeting George Harrison, Rolf and Cilla backstage afterwards. As a child, that was an awesome experience for me. I found the world of entertainment really inspirational. Even though, at the time, I didn't know who Cilla Black and the Beatles were, I was incredibly impressed by the entertainment business, and not for all the usual reasons. I just liked the people and their attitude. Of course, a couple of years later, back in Perth, it had an even greater impact when we started to see the Beatles and Cilla Black in Australia. I'd watch the shows and think Wow! I met them and I didn't even realize who they were.

Having first met Rolf in 1964, I saw him again a few years ago, when we happened to be sitting next to each other on an aeroplane in Australia. He was going to do a charity show, and I couldn't believe it, it seemed like fate. I spoke to him about my mother, who at that time was really ill, and we talked about my Aunt Jennifer, and he was very positive. I really appreciated that. He's a wonderful man.

I also told Rolf that when my eldest son, James, was born I'd asked my wife if we could call him Roll, but she didn't get it. It wasn't that Rolf was an idol of mine or anything like that, I just thought the name Roll Farris sounded good. Though I think James would have grown up as a different child if we had named him Roll!

The thing I've always loved about Rolf, and still do to this day, is his painting and drawing. It's his whole approach to it. I used to love watching him talk to his audience. He'd pull out a big canvas and do a huge painting on it. He constantly struck me as clever, the way he'd combine his painting with his singing and natural persona. He was a very gentle, warm man, and that impressed me, too. I've always been attracted to people like that. One day I'd love to buy one of his pictures, though I don't know if he ever sells them, or where I'd put it.

You would need a huge wall to hang an original Rolf Harris! But it's something I've wanted since I was a little boy, for no other reason than that I love them.

I've always felt, with Rolf, that he knew when he was on to a really good song, and that his personality went into his music. For me, the most important thing you need to possess to reach people is an attitude that comes through in your performance. Music isn't a sport. It's not about how good you are at playing your instrument; it's about what you convey with it. Music is about entertainment, and if you can entertain people when they're simply listening to you that's a wonderful thing to do. And the best way to do that is with tons of personality and attitude. The way Rolf sings songs like 'Two Little Boys' and 'Tie Me Kangaroo Down, Sport' shows that he has heaps of both.

There's an old saying in the music business here in Australia: 'England is a bitch!' No disrespect but, from an entertainment point of view, England can be a nightmare. So good on Rolf for sticking it out for so long!

TED EGAN

As District Officer for Aboriginal Affairs in the North of Australia, Ted Egan was assigned to look after Rolf and Alwen in the late Sixties when Rolf went walkabout in Arnhem Land, home to several tribes of native Aborigines. But Ted's influence on Rolf's career stretched much further than accompanying him in the outback.

In the late Sixties I received a message from Darwin that Rolf Harris was coming up to the Northern Territories to study Aboriginal culture. At the time I was based in north-east Arnhem Land, which is at the top of Australia, working for the Government at what was then called the Native Affairs Branch, in charge of Aboriginal administration in the region. As we were right out on the frontier, there were no hotels or motels, so we were asked to accommodate him, which, of course, we were delighted to do. Rolf and Alwen came out and they were very friendly. We took them camping in the bush, and Rolf did a few performances for the local Aboriginal community.

One night we were chatting and I said to him, 'I know an old song my mum taught me. I reckon if you recorded this you'd do well with it.'

Rolf replied, 'OK, sing it for me!'

So I started singing 'Two little boys had two little toys, each had a wooden horse ...'

Rolf's eyes glazed over; he probably thought it was a pretty corny song, but as I got to the line 'Did you think I would leave you dying' his eyes lit up. Rolf had, of all things, a tape recorder with him – in those days we had never seen such a thing. He pulled out this little magic machine and recorded me singing the song. We spent a few more cordial days out in the bush, swimming, talking and meeting Aborigines, then they went back to London.

Not long afterwards, Rolf phoned me from London and said, 'I can't get that "Two Little Boys" song out of my mind. I've organized to do it on my TV show next week and I can't find the bloody tape. I vaguely remember the sentiments of the song, but I can't remember the detail. Will you sing it for me over the phone?'

I said, 'You've got to be bloody joking.' But of course he persuaded me.

He performed it on his show, and it made an incredible impact. After that he recorded it, and in the end it pushed the Beatles off the top of the charts for about three months. It was the song of the year. Ever since then he has acknowledged that, had it not been for my mum remembering the song and singing it to me, it would almost certainly have died. We established that it was an American Civil War song, but the vast majority of Americans have never heard of it, and if they have it is probably only because they know Rolf's version.

Rolf has a wonderful affinity with people, and I have seen him do some beautiful things. I was with him once at the infamous Doyles restaurant in Sydney, which is a lovely place right on the beach. We were having lunch with a couple of friends when a fairly precocious

Popular Sixpenny Edition.

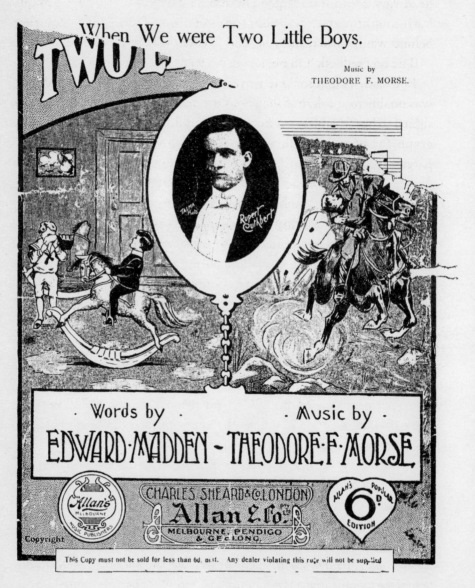

When We were Two Little Boys.

Music by
THEODORE F. MORSE.

· Words by ·   · Music by ·

EDWARD·MADDEN — THEODORE·F·MORSE

CHARLES SHEARD & Co LONDON
Allan & Co
MELBOURNE, BENDIGO
& GEELONG

Copyright

6^{D.}

This Copy must not be sold for less than 6d. nett.   Any dealer violating this rule will not be supplied ten-year-old boy came over and thrust a bit of paper in front of Rolf saying, 'Can I have an autograph?'

Rolf gave him a quizzical look, but he never just gives an autograph, he always does a little sketch and has a bit of a chat. He talked to this fairly monstrous little boy, taking the steam out of him a little. Hovering behind was his sister, and Rolf said, 'Would your sister like one?'

The boy replied, 'Oh no, she don't want one, she can't talk.'

Rolf said, 'Is that so?' He waved to the little girl, who was deaf. She was unable to speak, but she could use sign language, so Rolf expertly signed to her for about ten minutes. He did a very elaborate little autograph for her, and then went over and had a chat with the girl's parents. Typically of Rolf, he was well up on the latest techniques for people with hearing and speech difficulties, which he discussed with them. It was a very touching incident.

Rolf has a great affinity with Aboriginal people, particularly David Blanasi, an Aboriginal elder and one of the world's most prominent players of the didgeridoo. Rolf has been a key figure in helping the Aborigines take their music and culture out into the world. Through that he has assisted in developing a better understanding and acceptance of the indigenous population of our country. He may live in England, but he is acutely Australian and Rolf is always conscious of the real issues in his homeland, and he brings a very mature perspective to them.

DENNIS MURPHY

Dennis Murphy is a freelance television director based in Sydney, Australia. He has known Rolf and Bruce Harris, both personally and professionally, for over ten years. During this time he has directed and edited various documentaries, music and entertainment specials for them.

In February 1997 I was approached by Bruce Harris to direct and edit the documentary series *Bligh of the Bounty – World Navigator*. I jumped at the offer; the opportunity to tackle a project of substance and integrity with Rolf and Bruce Harris was irresistible. In Rolf's own words, 'Yeaaaahhhhhhhhh!'

The four-part series told the full story of William Bligh's life, from his birth to his role as navigator on Captain James Cook's third voyage, through to the ill-fated voyage, and mutiny, on the *Bounty*. The series detailed Bligh's horrific open-boat voyage after Fletcher Christian cast him and eighteen shipmates adrift and concluded with Bligh's role as governor of New South Wales, appointed to fight the entrenched corruption of the Rum Corps, and his subsequent demise back in England.

The programmes were both challenging and immensely satisfying to produce. With Rolf as host, his brother Bruce as writer and executive producer and Jon Matthews as director of photography, we filmed in the UK, Australia, Tenerife, Tahiti, Canada, Jamaica and Hawaii.

One of the many memorable incidents that gave me a unique insight into Rolf during filming occurred at a tiny airstrip located at Lockhart, an Aboriginal community over 400 kms north of Cairns in far north Queensland. We had just completed two demanding days of shooting on Restoration Island, where Bligh first made landfall on his open-boat voyage, and were returning to Cairns. Whilst waiting for the aircraft to arrive, Rolf befriended two Aboriginal boys, who were about ten years old and were about to make their first flight on an aircraft. Their obvious excitement, combined with their nervousness of the big white bloke with the beard and hat, was quickly forgotten as Rolf got down on his knees – a big effort as he is no longer as agile as he once was – and entertained the boys with sleight-of-hand magic tricks with a coin. Rolf soon had the boys entranced, with them hooting and giggling each time Rolf made the coin disappear. Their huge smiles obviously gave Rolf and the rest of us immense pleasure; however, the reaction of the boys' father was perhaps even more significant. Initially it was one of suspicion, then surprise and then genuine pleasure at the effect Rolf was having on the boys.

It made me think that, perhaps, with people like Rolf, with his knowledge and experience of indigenous Australian culture, reconciliation might just be possible.

3

PORTRAIT PAINTERS

As an artist, Rolf is quite unique. Renowned for both his cartoons and the enormous paintings he produces in minutes, almost everyone has a memory of seeing Rolf create a picture. Less well known, but no less impressive, are his photography and woodwork.

Encouraged to prove his art as a boy by both his father and his teachers, Rolf had his first formal training in the UK in 1952, when he attended the City and Guilds art school in Kennington, where he met his future wife, Alwen. He made real progress when he took lessons from Australian impressionist painter Hayward Veal, whose techniques inspired Rolf to develop his own approach. When Rolf first started doing drawings on children's TV in the Fifties he used black chalk on card. During the years that followed, he gradually progressed to painting on bigger surfaces, combining his own ideas with the techniques taught to him by Hayward, so that by the time he was presenting *The Rolf Harris Show* he was also producing his huge landscapes on twelve-by-nine-foot backdrops. Although Rolf made the creation of such paintings look almost effortless, a lot of behind-the-scenes thought and practice went into each of his pictures. Rolf would sometimes rehearse the paintings in full size as many as five times, always against the stopwatch, so that he could create them in his allotted time on *The Rolf Harris Show* each week.

TONY HART

At the same time as Rolf was performing on his children's cartoon pro-grammes, Tony Hart was presenting his own art shows, including Vision On *and* Take Hart. *But far from there being any rivalry between the two screen artists, there was a mutual respect and friendship that grew from their common love of art.*

I started in television in 1952. Rolf was a year or so behind me in that respect, though it didn't take him long to catch up. I remember seeing him first as a cartoonist and illustrator, but I discovered fairly early on that he was a remarkable painter. One of the most brilliant pieces I've

AFTER BUT NOT QUITE CATCHING UP WITH

ever seen is a *Bottlescape* by Rolf, which is owned by George Martin, who is a mutual friend of ours.

I recall once when we were at the old Dickinson Road Studio in Manchester, when the studio was 'at rest'. There were only the usual dimmed bulbs on, but for some unknown reason there were blue and red lights shining into the room. These lights, along with the dimmed ones, were reflected in the highly polished top of the grand piano. Rolf noticed it and said, 'Look at that. Look at the colours in there! My goodness, I wish I had my brushes here, that would make a great picture.' And I knew exactly what he meant: it would be abstract, but it would have made a wonderful picture. Rolf has a painter's vision. I'm sure he has some pictures in galleries, and I think he's had exhibitions at places like the National, but truthfully we don't see enough of Rolf's paintings. I always thought that Rolf was a painter and I was a graphics man, though Rolf, of course, does cartoons very quickly, so he's a graphics man as well. But I wouldn't describe myself as a real painter; my compositions are coloured drawings. That's the difference between a real painter and somebody like me. He was always very sweet, though, and complimented me on my drawings.

We used to talk about painting and his style. I recollect him telling me that he thought a painting should never have too much detail in it, and certainly his paintings don't have the fine lines he saves for his drawing. He told me, 'If I feel I'm getting too much detail in a painting I take my glasses off and go on from there.' And he was so right, because I wear glasses some of the time. When I take them off and blink, things are out of focus, and if you are able to copy that out-of-focus perspective the result can look brilliant.

After I had got to know Rolf quite well, at a time when we were doing similar things on television, I met up with him one day. On his show Rolf did very large pictures with a distemper brush, and on my show, *Vision On*, I also did large pictures, only mine were with a tennis court marker on deserted airfields, making white-line drawings. Sometimes I wanted to do big pictures in the studio, so I said to Rolf, 'I know you use this great big brush to do these drawings, so I certainly won't do that.'

Rolf was so generous, he said, 'Oh, do that if you want to.'

I said, 'No, I can't do that, because that's your signature, but I'll tell you what I will do, if you don't mind, I'll use a paint roller.'

He said, 'Oh, great!' or words to that effect, which was so magnanimous.

I remember Rolf talking to my wife, Jean, at a party once. He had watched me painting a tiger on some black paper on TV, by putting in only the white bits. As the tiger evolved he obviously believed it was going to be unrecognizable and was quite concerned. Of course, within the last thirty seconds, I added the final all-important lines and it worked. He said to Jean, 'I really thought Tony had lost himself there, but he did it.' Of course, he was a master at that technique, and it was always so exciting to see what would evolve as he whistled and painted away.

Rolf and I once worked together on a show. When I was making *Vision On* I had an idea to invite Rolf on to the programme to play a game of musical-chair painting. I thought it would be great fun to have a large background and for each of us to start drawing a picture to music. When the music stopped we would rush over to the other's painting and carry it on. Although Rolf loved the idea, unfortunately it never came to fruition on my show. But several years later, when he was working on *Rolf's Cartoon Club*, he invited me down to Bristol and said, 'You remember that idea of yours for doing the musical drawing?'

I replied, 'Yes, I certainly do. Are we going to do that now?'

'Why not?' he asked, and we did it there and then. He started off with a head of a man, and I started with a pig's head. It ended up like that old parlour game, Head, Bodies and Clothes, which we used to play at Christmas.

JOHN BELLANY

John Bellany is a successful Scottish artist who has been a close friend of Rolf's and Alwen's since he met them in the early 1980s.

In 1983, Clifton Pugh, the Australian artist, was over in London with his girlfriend, staying just round the corner from Kensington Palace. They had a small dinner party one evening with Mark McManus – the actor who played Taggart – his wife and Rolf and Alwen Harris. I remember it was a fairly heavy night, great fun, with lots of singing. It was a wonderful evening and the next day I said to Rolf, 'Why don't you come across with Clifton and his girlfriend to the studio and we'll all paint each other.' Clifton and I had done this in Australia several times, so we got out various materials. I found an old bit of hardboard for Rolf, but he gave up on it and ended up doing a huge drawing on the wall of my studio. It was a picture of a story he had been telling about Jimmy Shand, the great Scottish accordionist.

We had quite a busy day of it; you can imagine what a ridiculous carry-on it was. At about three o'clock I suggested we join a Christmas party I knew was taking place at an East End pub, where various artist friends of mine were gathering. We drove across London and, when we got there, all my old pals were pretty well on the road to oblivion. We were having a great time when someone came up to Rolf and asked, 'Are you a Rolf Harris lookalike?' Rolf wasn't impressed at all, and started to sing all his songs to establish that he was the *real* Rolf. Once he'd proved himself they asked him to sign a ten-pound note for their children, and he ended up signing loads of five- and ten-pound notes. It turned into another smashing jamboree, just like the night before had been. That was my first encounter with Rolf and it was a great start to our friendship.

For my fiftieth birthday Rolf gave me an accordion. He came for lunch and brought Alwen, Bindi and one of Bindi's friends, who had a little boy. Our granddaughter was with us, and the two children got down to drawing almost immediately. Rolf and I joined in the session and my granddaughter, who is usually quite shy about drawing, really came to life. Later, we were out in the garden playing the accordion to each other and singing duets for ages. It was a very memorable day.

Rolf's drawings are much better than anything else he does because they are done so freely. When he draws people he gets a good likeness, and he loves it. You can see there is so much love in his drawings. He's drawn all our family, and there's an intensity to the pictures that is quite remarkable. Rolf's daughter, Bindi, is an excellent painter. Since leaving art school she has gone from strength to strength. And, of course, Alwen is a great artist, too. She is the rock the Harris family is built on, and Bindi has a very similar personality to Alwen. They are a very tight-knit, happy family.

As well as having many happy times together, Rolf has shared our hard times. Some years ago I was in St Thomas's Hospital for a long stretch. My liver had packed up, and at the time there were very few transplants available. I thought I was on my last legs and was very down. I was lying in a hospital bed, with my wife beside me holding my hand. My mind was mulling over serious issues, like life and death, when I heard a faint noise in the distance. It sounded like an accordion, miles away, and I thought, Ach, I'm just dreaming. But it got nearer and nearer, very quiet, very gentle, and then the accordion came into the room, a wee bit louder, but still gentle. I opened my eyes and there was Rolf, standing at the foot of my bed playing the accordion. He and Alwen had come to visit, and for me it was so moving. He was play-ing Scottish songs, and it really bucked me up. When they left, my wife said I was looking a lot more like my usual self. It was such an important moment for me, at a time when I genuinely believed I was on my way out. In the event, I did receive a transplant, and thirteen years later I'm still here! After I'd recovered, I did a painting of the scene with Rolf, Alwen and my wife. It has a sign above my head, which says, 'Nil by mouth', and it's now in an American collection in New York. It's a sad painting because of the poignancy of the situ-ation, but it has happiness in it as well, which is a great tribute to Rolf.

Most recently, in 1995, we were with Rolf the day before he went on *This is Your Life*. Obviously he didn't know he was going to be on it, and neither did we. As far as he knew, all he was doing the next day was leading a band of pipers along Princes Street. Although I say *all*, I should point out that this was to be the biggest band of pipers ever gathered together at one time, over 3,000 of them, in fact! The day before he confided in me that he was a little nervous. 'I must admit,' he said, 'I'm really worried about it. I'll tell you what it is, I don't think I've got enough puff to last out.'

I said to him, 'Look, your worries are over. It's simple. All you have to do is get an onion, cut it in two and, when the thing starts, you slip the half an onion in your mouth. Your cheeks will puff out, and it'll look as if you're blowing like anything. On top of that, there'll be thousands of pipers there. It's not as if you're going to be heard among that crowd!'

The next day, he was supposed to be coming to see us immediately after the march up Princes Street. We were waiting for his arrival when we received a phone call from Alwen saying, 'Rolf's on *This is Your Life* and we're being flown to London right away!'

I said, 'How did he get on with the onion?' Alwen didn't know what I was talking about, so hopefully he didn't put my suggestion into practice, otherwise he would have met all the guests with polluted breath!

PETER MURPHY

Peter Murphy worked with Rolf between 1987 and 1993 on Rolf's Cartoon Club *for HTV, during which time they recorded over 120 shows. Peter was not only the programme's executive producer, he formed a creative team with Rolf that shaped the show from the beginning.*

Rolf first approached HTV in 1987 when his BBC show, *Rolf Harris Cartoon Time*, had run its course. He felt the programme had got to a point where it was no longer breaking new ground, and he didn't feel there was any commitment, investment or creative input going into the show. All the BBC really wanted Rolf to do was wear his Hawaiian shirt, sit at an easel, draw a character and link into the cartoons.

At that time the legendary Billy Marsh was representing Rolf, and he set up an initial meeting for us. From the first moment we met we clicked. We discussed the fact that if we were going to pitch a new programme to ITV we needed a new concept, and *Rolf's Cartoon Club* was what we came up with.

We created a unique setting for the show, with a cockpit in the studio. Our aim was to get as far away as possible from the kind of show *Cartoon Time* had been. To help with that, we got Rolf to work on-screen with children. Strangely enough, that was something he had never done before; even the *Young Generation* were adults, albeit youthful ones. We created a club for viewers to join, and they signed up in their thousands. Essentially, what we set out to do was open up the world of animation. We brought in specialists, animators and a wonderful producer-director called Doug Wilcox. Between us we created a format where we could show how cartoons were produced, and in each programme we had a children's animation workshop, where they could try out different animation techniques and work on their own ideas.

We not only showed classic cartoons, such as the Warner Brothers and Disney, in our 'Showcase' section of the show, we also showed unusual material from around the globe. We were the first show to invite Nick Park on, quite some time before he became successful. Nobody had seen *Wallace & Gromit* in those days; Nick was still beavering away in his little studio in Bristol. *Rolf's Cartoon Club* was interesting in so many ways, not least because it premiered unique and different animation from around the world.

Over the years we developed new spots in the show for celebrity guests to join Rolf. The who's who of the animation world appeared on the show, bringing in the original designs and drawings of their characters. We had Tony Hart guesting, and for the first time the two legends painted a wall together. We even went to Hollywood for a Christmas special, and Rolf met some of his own animation heroes, such as Chuck Jones and Friz Freeleng. As the years progressed, Nick Park became a regular guest, even bringing in his Oscar, and each time we would flash back to his first appearance on the show as an unknown.

Rolf had wanted a show to give him a new lease of life, and *Cartoon Club* gave him something that grew beyond all expectations. Rolf absolutely adored doing the show, and he was such an animated character himself. He was also incredibly committed. At seven o'clock in the morning he could regularly be found in the graphics studio at HTV, making wonderful compositions that would be built into the show. He made things like mobiles, which were wonderful works of art and were used to illustrate items. At the end of the day, the children who had appeared with him would each get an individually drawn cartoon of their own from Rolf. Then he'd return to the graphics studio and do some more work for the next day. My first and lasting impression of Rolf is of an absolutely dedicated professional. He is a total artist, in the widest sense of the word.

Because Rolf's art is so popular and instant, I don't think society has truly recognized what he is capable of. He makes what he's doing look so easy, but Rolf is actually a remarkable painter. He has exhibited his paintings at the Royal Academy, and there's a whole side to Rolf that people don't see on television. However, where television is concerned he is a genius. To watch Rolf work to camera is to see a master at work. I often say to younger presenters, 'If you want to learn how to work to camera, watch Rolf Harris.' Interestingly, I don't think Rolf originally thought there would be such an opportunity to take children through the animation world without destroying the magic of it, but he gave the show a depth, integrity and dimension that inspired a lot of children to go to art college and on into the animation world.

Unfortunately, all good things must come to an end. They were wonderful years, when I developed a great friendship with Rolf, and we all knew we'd done something special. But in 1993, when a new commissioner of programmes took over, ITV decided not to re-commision the show. Rolf was heartbroken. But, as I have said to him since, and I know Lorraine Heggessey from the BBC agrees with me, there is an element of fate to these things. If *Cartoon Club* hadn't stopped when it did, Rolf wouldn't have been available to do *Animal Hospital*.

MAC

In 1999 Mac was awarded the British Press Award for Cartoonist of the Year. He has worked at the Daily Mail *for many years, and in that time Mac has used Rolf Harris as a subject for some of his cartoons, most recently on the occasion of Australia's referendum about remaining in the Commonwealth.*

My interest in Rolf was first aroused in the early Sixties when he came over to England and sang 'Tie Me Kangaroo Down, Sport' with his wobble-board. It was a fabulous song, and he came over as a wonderful personality. I've always enjoyed Rolf on the television. I think he is extraordinarily talented, and his bubbling enthusiasm comes right across the airwaves when you watch him.

When I first saw Rolf do his amazingly huge drawings with a couple of paintbrushes in his hand, I immediately went out to my garage and tried it myself. I used an enormous piece of board, but didn't get anywhere near as good a result, so I was always full of admiration for his technique and ability on such a large scale. I tried it again when I was wallpapering a room once. I painted some large pictures before I put the wallpaper up. Some time later I moved house and received a call from the new occupant. He said, 'I've found your obscene drawings under the wallpaper we've just stripped off!'

As a cartoonist I think Rolf is terrific. His cartoons are immediate; he draws them so swiftly and the ideas seem to flow from his mind instantaneously. My style is very different. I try to think of something

'It's alright. They've seen sense – you can release Rolf Harris.'

topical, and then laboriously draw it up for the next morning's paper. I love the spontaneity and slickness of Rolf's cartoons.

ZOË JELLEY

Zoë Jelley, a professional photographer, and her husband, Gordon, are close friends of Rolf and Alwen.

We met Rolf and Alwen at the infamous Pikes Hotel in Ibiza. Knowing it was where Freddy Mercury had holidayed, and Elton John had held his fortieth birthday party, we arrived in anticipation, wondering which celebrities might be among the guests during our stay, apart from us, of course!

We asked the head waiter at dinner on our first night and he replied, "Ave you ever 'eard of Rolf 'Arris?' We had, but was this the best they could do? (Only joking Rolf!) The next morning was very exciting when who should be in reception but the man himself, along with the lovely Alwen. It was even better when they invited us to join them for dinner that evening. We soon discovered that we had much in common, including animals, photography, woodwork, jewellery-making, eating – trenchermen make the best guests – not to mention singing loudly in public places!

Rolf often invites me along with my camera to document different aspects of his work, of which there are many. The most memorable event I have accompanied him on was his performance at Glastonbury in 1998. The atmosphere was magical, in spite of the mud, and his reception on stage was astounding. The photos came out pretty well, too!

Rolf always has time for his fans, never turns anyone away and always shows an interest in what they have to say. I think a lady at an *Animal Hospital* roadshow summed it up for me when she told a story about her grandchild who, when asked at school who was the patron saint of animals, replied, 'Rolf Harris.'

Bruce and Rolf Harris, alias Tom Sawyer and Huckleberry Finn, in Bassendean, 1940.

Rolf taking some back-seat driving lessons from Mum, while Dad sensibly opts for the safety of his bike.

Rolf with his mum, Marge, and dad, Crom.

Rolf freshly arrived in London, beard-free, minus the specs and wearing a tie. Definitely a one-off!

Australia's junior backstroke champion, 1946. Aquarius

Having sung for his fare, Rolf stands proudly with the rest of the Western Australia team on his way to Melbourne for the Australian National Swimming Championships. (Rolf is the one with his initial protruding from his head.)

Auditioning for the national radio show, *Australia's Amateur Hour*, Rolf performs 'Seven Beers With the Wrong Woman' in his inimitable style.

Hats off to Sydney! At the Sydney Opera House during its construction. In 1973 Rolf performed at the completed concert hall's inaugural show.

No doubt about it, Rolf certainly has style.

Courtesy Burt Coleman

Rolf trying to stand on his own three feet.

Singing the wobble-board's praises.

Getting a hand from the mischievous Coojeebear.

Rolf on clap sticks, David Blanasi on didgeridoo and Bindi Harris on finger.

'On your marks, get set, go...' Rolf cuts the ribbon for Phab at the Warrington Disability Awareness Day, 1998.

Zoë Jelley

What's that noise? Rolf preparing to lead over 3,000 pipers up Princes Street, Edinburgh, in aid of Marie Curie Cancer Research.

Buttons enjoying a private panto moment with Lorraine Chase as Cinders.

RH meets HRH with Tommy Cooper after a Royal Command performance. Just like that!

They seek him here, they Secombe there. Rolf and Alwen relish gooning around with close friend Harry.

'Now stop me if you've heard this before...' Rolf and Parky enjoy a very public conversation.

Rolf and Alwen,
with bridesmaid Pugsy,
on their wedding day
in 1958.

On the beach – Rolf, Bindi
and Alwen Harris, 1966.

Another magical moment was the Aboriginal corroboree at the Union Chapel, Islington, in 1999. Hundreds of didgeridoo players descended on London from all over the world to see Rolf playing with his mentor, David Blanasi, and also to join in playing alongside him. The sound was incredible.

4

MINSTRELS IN THE GALLERY

Prior to the release of 'Stairway to Heaven' Rolf had always relied on a musical director, who would accompany him with a caseful of music sheets and rehearse local musicians to perform his shows. He had never had his own backing band, apart from the short-lived Digaroos, with whom he toured briefly in 1963 following the release of 'Sun Arise'. However, after the success of 'Stairway to Heaven' and the subsequent regular concert performances at colleges round the country, it was appropriate that the music stands were dispensed with and a regular band was established to back Rolf. That band sprang from the session musicians who were hastily assembled for the TV promotion of 'Stairway to Heaven', and, with the exception of a couple of sabbaticals, the band has remained the same ever since.

For much of Rolf's career, Barry Booth toured the world with Rolf as his musical director. But before Barry, and long before Robert Plant and Jimmy Page had even formed Led Zeppelin, let alone written 'Stairway to Heaven', Laurie Holloway took care of the music.

LAURIE HOLLOWAY

Laurie Holloway is currently musical director for Parkinson. *He has worked with Rolf on many occasions, performing on a number of his records and enjoying a long stint as Rolf's musical director in the Sixties.*

I started working with Rolf through a bass player named Spike Heatley. Rolf was putting a band together for a live radio show, and Spike recommended me as the piano player. We had a great time on the broadcasts. Rolf used to turn up with a stack of chord sheets; we never had proper music scores. The show ran for several years and was very successful; we also performed at shows like *Talk of the Town*. Ever since those early days Rolf and I have got on famously, both musically and socially.

Rolf has always enjoyed humour that revolves around misuse of language. In the band we had a guitar player called George Kish, who was Hungarian. Rolf and I used to derive great mirth from George. He had come to Britain in 1956, during the revolution, and he'd never quite mastered the English language. Rolf and my quartet, of which George was a member, used to broadcast the show every week. One day George arrived ten minutes late. He walked in and said, 'Sorry I'm late, I could have been earlier!' Rolf and I fell about with laughter.

George also used to get his Ws and Vs mixed up. One time he said, 'I just bought a new car, I got a Wolwo!' So I said, 'Why didn't you get a Wauxhall Wiwa?' And he replied, 'Ah, my vife doesn't like them!'

Rolf was always into his strange instruments, even then. He was always wobbling his wobble-board, which I didn't mind, but I hated the Stylophone. It was a horrible noise, though I couldn't tell him that! He was so enthusiastic about the thing that I didn't want to puncture his bubble.

Several years ago Rolf and Alwen became neighbours of ours. I'm madly in love with Alwen! I've known her as long as I've known Rolf and she's outrageous, a wonderful character. In many ways she complements Rolf. They both never pretend to be something they are not, and there's no big-time attitude to either Alwen or Rolf.

BARRY BOOTH

From the end of the Sixties, when Rolf was at number one with 'Two Little Boys', right through to the beginning of the Nineties, Barry Booth was Rolf's musical director, travelling with him around the world.

Soon after I began working with Rolf, I became at first astonished and then impressed by the extraordinary amount of time and energy he devotes to charitable work. Naturally, I welcomed the opportunity to accompany Rolf every Christmas to one or other of the many children's hospital wards he visits, where some of the young patients were very unwell indeed. To witness those young faces, filled with delight, as Rolf enchanted them with a story, a song and some clowning was truly epiphanic. It's magical to watch youngsters getting a right good cheering up, a real 'Rolfing'! It's efficacious for the soul.

One Christmas Day we travelled to a nightclub in Bedfordshire to give a lunchtime performance for an audience of hundreds of children, the vast majority of whom were from children's homes. Show time arrived and I made my way onto the stage where a grand piano stood. I struck up Rolf's intro music — the old familiar one, two, oom-pah, oom-pah. Rolf began his entry onto the stage: that famous up-and-down, comical trudge so appropriate for the persona of Jake the Peg. In my view it's one of the best opening routines in showbiz.

Hundreds of kids, bursting with anticipation and Christmas pud, erupted into an unholy cacophony of screaming and applause. Moments later, Rolf passed the piano on his way to centre stage, a follow-spot highlighting his every move. Suddenly I heard a gasp from the audience and became aware that some of them were

shrieking with laughter and pointing at Rolf. He turned to me and I caught the expression on his face – not easy to describe – a wondrous mixture of helplessness and urgency. To further my appreciation of his predicament, I peered round the body of the Steinway and saw – oh calamity! – Jake's extra leg lying on its side at Rolf's feet. I watched in hysterics as, bending at the knees, he extended his usually concealed right hand below the hem of Jake's coat to retrieve the lost property, all the while dying a thousand deaths (the eternal dread of those in peril on the stage). The mystery surrounding Jake the Peg's extra leg melted away on that particular day for those particular children and, years later, I still cherish the memory of Rolf's expression as he turned to look at me after disaster struck. Priceless!

Remembering that children's party reminds me of the first time we played Carnegie Hall. At the band call in the afternoon we met the musicians who would back the show at the evening performance – all top-class New York session men and very seasoned professionals. The rehearsal was trouble free, and no-one batted an eyelid as we explained some of the unusual things Rolf would do in his show. These guys were unfazable. The legendary Lee Morgan was on trumpet and he expressed an interest in the didgeridoo; Rolf later sent him one as a gift. Above all, I was struck by the craggy, impassive face of the man on sax; such a forbidding countenance. Would he never smile? So you can imagine my delight when the show began and Rolf appeared as Jake the Peg in full costume, sporting the famous extra leg. Our ultracool sax man was almost on the floor in paroxysms of mirth and was quite unable to play. And he thought he'd seen it all!

Rolf understands his audiences perfectly. What his fans love is for Rolf to share his unique mindset with them and tell them stuff in his inimitable way. Even the cleverest of impressionists don't really get close to the essence. Rolf is a consummate master of yarn-spinning; there is simply none finer. I have watched him night after night for literally thousands of performances and have never ceased to be amazed by the precision of his delivery. It all seems so effortless that you might easily overlook the finely honed techniques of timing and inflection. He has a phenomenal ear for the subtle intricacies of spoken language and characterization. Arty-farty music could do nothing to enhance the quality of his performance; in fact, it would most likely be an impediment. Almost without exception his famous songs consist of powerful narrative threads, the musical settings of which are carefully and craftily designed, existing simply to support the unfolding of the stories. The tale-telling is the thing that matters most.

In a similar way, Rolf ingeniously subverts the whole business of picture painting into a narrative-based performance art form. Each painting progresses through its various stages – exposition, development and diversionary episodes – until the moment of denouement arrives and the audience is invited to speculate and decipher the plot, after which, with a few deft strokes of his four-inch distemper brush, Rolf gleefully reveals the surprising finale. All the while, during this exercise, he will regale the audience with a continuous stream of comments, anecdotes and hot one-liners. Again, it is Rolf's artful technique that masks the complexity of what he is doing. He makes it all look so easy.

SIMON BATES

Many people were surprised and delighted when Rolf had his massive hit in 1993 with Led Zeppelin's tour de force, 'Stairway to Heaven', not least the man himself. The subsequent rise of Rolf to cult student icon in the aftermath of its release is the stuff of legends. Despite its being an obvious hit, Rolf's record company, Polygram, was originally hesitant to release it in the UK. It was only after an unprecedented amount of radio airplay on Simon Bates's Radio 1 show that it was released, and from that moment Rolf's live concerts would never be the same.

My enjoyment of Rolf Harris goes back a few years to 1980. There was an annual tradition for a group of us to go to the Rolf Harris pantomime, wherever he was appearing. There was a hard-core party who always came – ex-news and BBC current-affairs people, a few people from ITV, ITN and some of the Radio 1 crowd. We would make up a party, hire a charabanc and go to see Rolf in pantomime; they were hysterical shows and worked on so many different levels.

Then, in the early Nineties, a mate of mine from the Australian Broadcasting Commission rang me up and said, 'Rolf Harris has done a version of "Stairway to Heaven"!'

I said, 'Don't be silly, you're wasting my time!'

But he persisted: 'No. Honestly, we've just done "Stairway to Heaven" with Rolf Harris, and you will not believe it!' He sent me a tape of the programme, *The Money or the Gun*. It was such a brilliant concept: getting the special guest who appeared on the show each week to do a version of 'Stairway to Heaven'. I thought it was inspired. I watched the video of Rolf doing his rendition, and it was so wonderful and funny. Rolf was singing the song, but obviously didn't understand what he was getting involved in.

I played the tape on Radio 1 every day, and eventually Rolf's record company got involved. They were beginning to lose interest in Rolf as a recording artist at the time, and only seemed to want to put out reissues. It was coming up to Christmas, and our fear was that they would re-release 'Two Little Boys'. Anything but that!

'Stairway To Heaven' is a great example of Australian irony. Rolf actually told me that he didn't even know who Led Zeppelin were when he got involved. To Rolf, whom I don't know well but have always admired, I suspect it was a bunch of lyrics and a piece of music. He probably said, 'All right, I'll do that,' without a fuss, which, of course, is a very Australian attitude. I know quite a few people who performed on the television series, and they all performed the song on the same basis. Australians look at these things in a different way. There was a tango version, an Elvis version, opera and all sorts. They don't care how sacred a song is, they just go for it, which I think is a great attitude to have towards music.

And, of course, the song has had a wonderful effect on his concert career. I've been to a couple of his university gigs, and I couldn't believe all the shouting and waving going on, with Rolf up there looking slightly puzzled, but loving every minute of it. I think that sometimes he doesn't actually understand the audience's reaction, but that's the joy of it. The audience sings every word with him; songs of that kind – popular music in the classic sense – are like nursery rhymes. Everyone knows the verse and chorus of 'Jake the Peg' and 'Two Little Boys'; they're in the national psyche. And Rolf Harris is in the national psyche, too.

BOB CLIFFORD

When Polygram were putting out 'Stairway to Heaven' as a single, Bob Clifford was asked by Rolf to help put a band together for TV promotion. Rolf's version of the song features all his individual trademarks, including wobble-board, didgeridoo and a subtle play on the original lyrics, creating the character Miss Given from the line 'All of our thoughts are misgiven'. Her role in the song involves strutting on stage and swapping Rolf's wobble-board for his didgeridoo!

Rolf's songs have been published by EMI Music, or one of its sister companies, since the Fifties. Having myself worked for EMI since the late Seventies, I've got to know Rolf well. He is loved within the company, and will occasionally pop into the offices and draw on the walls!

In December 1992 I received a message to call Rolf, and when I returned it he explained that he had recorded a version of 'Stairway to Heaven' for an Australian TV show. It was being released in the UK through Phonogram (part of Polygram), and the original band he'd used was back in Australia. Would I help him get a band together to do the promotion work on the single? Being an OK guitarist – my modesty doesn't allow me to elaborate on my plucking prowess – I volunteered myself and said I would rustle up some more fine musicians.

I knew Mick Gaffey as an ex-EMI songwriter and consummate

drummer, not to mention a very nice man, and I knew he would enjoy being in Rolf's band of merry men. My next call was to Danny Thompson, probably the finest double-bass player in the country. He was busy, but suggested Bernard O'Neill – probably the second finest. Rolf's contacts at Phonogram suggested a keyboard player from Bob Geldof's band, who also played the accordion, Alan Dunn. Alan knew Bernard, and so the band was born.

We all met up on 2 February 1993 at a small rehearsal room that I had arranged for Phonogram. The band valiantly played through my rough chord charts, with Rolf suggesting plenty of performance details, for example, talking us through when Miss Given would come on. The room was booked for three hours, but within an hour we had all emerged smiling and happy.

In the early afternoon three days later we met up again, this time at a TV studio in Wembley; the single was starting to get great radio airplay and we were scheduled to appear on *The Word* – at last my kids would appreciate that I was hip! We arrived at the studio to be greeted by members of the crew on their knees, bowing to Rolf and wailing, 'We're not worthy, we're not worthy,' in *Wayne's World* stylee. As we weren't miming – it was all to be nail-bitingly live – we had a lengthy run-through, followed by a rest, a little musical jamming session with Rolf – who proved to be no slouch on the accordion himself – an Indian meal, with Rolf recounting tales of yore, and then back to the studio to await our cue. It all went rather well, with Rolf on fine form. For us, the thought of millions of people watching somehow enhanced the performance, and the lovely Nikki from Phonogram wandering on as Miss Given helped considerably!

The next week I took a day off work as we motored up to Liverpool together for Richard and Judy's *This Morning*. We visited the Beatles Story Exhibition around the corner from the studios between setting up and broadcasting time and discovered that Rolf had done various shows with the Beatles in the early Sixties. It was also our first taste of Rolf's autograph-signing prowess.

The following day we filmed *Top of the Pops*. Much to the consternation of the studio staff, we performed it live without a backing track, so they had to hunt around for spare microphones and monitors, muttering, 'Sorry, guv, we've run out; we don't get many live acts on the show these days!' The BBC studios are only a stone's throw from where I live, so my wife, Sue, joined our happy crew and, in between the soundcheck and the show, we wandered round Albert Square and watched Rolf teach a member of a heavy-metal band how to do circular breathing!

The show was wonderful and the single steamed up the charts. As we left the studio, with our instruments in our hands, a Dutch TV crew filmed us playing in the corridor; it was later broadcast on Dutch TV.

That was my tenure with the Rolf Harris Band. He did ask me if I could perform at his live shows, but I have a day job – a career some would say – so sadly had to decline, thereby missing his triumph at Glastonbury. So it goes, but I have fantastic memories of those three great TV shows with Uncle Rolf. And with the extra cash I bought myself a rather nice acoustic guitar! Thanks *The Word*, *This Morning*, *TOTP*, Phonogram, Led Zep . . . but mostly, thanks, Rolf!

BERNARD O'NEILL

A native of Dublin, Bernard O'Neill has been Rolf's musical director since 'Stairway to Heaven'. Together with Rolf and the other three musicians quickly assembled to promote the single, he saw at first hand Rolf's elevation to student icon and cult hero on the live circuit. He has also been instrumental in helping Rolf evolve from his cabaret days, and here he recounts how that progression took place.

I had been working with famous acts for several years when I first met Rolf, so I wasn't awe-struck. But I was surprised by Rolf's immediacy, and the fact that he was exactly the same in the flesh as he is on the television. He isn't a media person putting on an act; he is simply himself. That pleased me more than anything else because, like many of the people who work with him, we had grown up with Rolf through our childhood. In fact, the only difference I perceived in Rolf from my childhood image of him was that he was a little bit greyer.

I remember all Rolf's shows involving a high degree of levity. His contemporaries in that field would either try to be funny and fail, in my eyes, or they seemed to be very staid and safe. Rolf, however, was always funny. I remember one particular show when he came on stage and played electric guitar very badly. Of course, now I know why, because to this day he cannot fathom stringed instruments to save his life!

In every other area, however, Rolf is a very fine musician. He actually knows an awful lot about music and comes from a generation that grew up with strongly held views about music. Though, to his credit, Rolf can be very irreverent in some ways. I'll never forget the first time I played Led Zeppelin's version of 'Stairway to Heaven' for him. It was the first time he had ever heard it properly, and his reaction was, 'Oh no, what have I done?'

Rolf's previous musical directors have been phenomenal, like Laurie Holloway and Barry Booth. They are very cerebral musicians and very good arrangers who come from the old school. When the new band started with Rolf in 1993, his set had hardly altered in thirty years.

It soon became apparent that things would have to change pretty quickly. Rolf had never been on stage with us, although we had done five or six television shows with him and rehearsed up his cabaret set. When we arrived at Birmingham University for the first gig, there was a sound system that would probably be OK in a small club, but not in a room with a capacity of 600. We were billed to go on at ten o'clock. At about half-past eight the place was teeming, with 1,800 people in the room, all roaring for Rolf.

Backstage, Rolf said, 'Let's go on now.' To which I replied, 'No way, they'll eat you for dinner!' When we did play it was honestly not dissimilar to the Beatles playing Shea Stadium. We emerged on stage and couldn't hear a thing; the audience screamed constantly for fifteen minutes. Rolf looked at me as if to say, What are we going to do? But all we could do was perform the set. Throughout the show we couldn't hear a word he sang and he couldn't hear us; we didn't even know where we were in the song most of the time. Afterwards, when we went into the dressing room, Rolf was elated; we were scraping him off the ceiling! The students lined up outside, and he eventually got out at two in the morning. They hugged and kissed him and helped him pack his car. There were literally hundreds of people, all clamouring for Rolf. But it was such a buzz; it was incredible, like being at the beginning of the Beatles again.

A few days later, when the excitement had died down a bit, I said, 'We're going to have to rethink this, Rolf!' And that was when the band went electric. Stories went round the universities and colleges like wild fire that Rolf was a crazy man with a great band doing crazy things. That year was totally outrageous. But it was also a real learning curve, because Rolf had never played with a regular band before. He'd always had a musical director, and had relied on him to take charge of the backing musicians reading his music. He didn't know quite how much to trust us at first, especially when we altered his old material and rocked it up. But as time progressed, I think he became more confident of what we were doing, and felt it was appropriate for his new-found audience.

I remember George Martin saying to me, 'When you record with Rolf, you have to remember that Rolf's voice is the selling part. You can't have him moving too far away from what he is just because it's a rock song.' So, with all the new material we've worked on since the band came together, there has been a compromise between giving some integrity to the song and making sure it's still Rolf. The greatest compliment is that songwriters who have had their songs covered by Rolf love them. I was told that Edwyn Collins went out and bought Rolf's album *Can You Tell What it is Yet?* because he loved Rolf's version of 'A Girl Like You'. So it cuts both ways; there has been a big change, but Rolf has understood that the transition was necessary, and he has gradually accepted it.

There have been some fantastic moments over the last few years. I remember an incident in Sheffield when Rolf went off stage after Jake the Peg, ripped off the costume but forgot to remove his trousers. He ran back out on stage still wearing his three-legged bright orange trousers with a safety pin on the fly, and proceeded to go straight into the next number, with me shouting at him, 'Get your strides off!'

The best experience of all was probably the Glastonbury main stage in 1993, where we had an estimated 84,000 people watching; it was simply awesome. I'd got down there very early because there was a production meeting for the musical directors. We'd been hanging around with various other bands backstage, then suddenly it was time to go on, and the noise was just incredible. It was brilliant; it really was an amazing experience.

Working with Rolf has been a privilege, especially when we have worked with him in other situations, seeing other areas of his talent. When we performed on *The National Lottery Show* with Rolf, he did six large paintings through the course of the afternoon during the various rehearsals in a very short space of time. Watching him, it occurred to me that if I were simply to try to whitewash the same space it would take me at least as long as it took him to do a painting.

GRAEME TAYLOR

A founder member of groups such as Gryphon, The Albion Band and Home Service, Graeme Taylor is one of Britain's most respected folk guitarists. As one of his original influences was a certain Rolf Harris, it seems fitting that he now performs regularly alongside the man himself.

I remember, as a child in the early Sixties, sitting in front of our very new TV set, avidly soaking up the wrestling, *Dr Who, Thank Your Lucky Stars* and, later, the much-anticipated *Rolf Harris Show*.

Is *that* what a Fijian girl looks like?

One night, the big song was 'Fijian Girl', and Rolf magically created a black-and-white painting live in the studio – all TV was live in those days – of a tropical island scene that still exists to this day in my memory in full technicolor. It was around 1967, in a large exercise book, that I attempted to recreate the whole scenario – pictures, lyrics, guitar chords and all. My parents had recently bowed to increased pressure, via my obsession with the Beatles, to include a five-pound guitar in that year's Christmas sack. Little did they suspect the consequences.

I got the verse worked out perfectly, but foundered entirely on the middle-eight section, where a succession of beautiful and very clever modulations of key occur. However, thirty-four years later, magically, I found myself in a big professional recording studio with the man himself, recording the same song for real. Much to Rolf's delight, I think I'd just about sorted out that middle eight by then!

Rolf will bend over backwards to please his audience, whatever their provenance. We played the Welsh National Anthem in Cardiff, 'Danny Boy' in Dublin and 'The Flowers of Scotland' in Glasgow, with Rolf adorned in a kilt and tam-o'-shanter provided inspirationally by a particularly shapely Govan wench. Rolf's eyes were popping! In one gig alone we played six different national anthems, completely unrehearsed and completely inaccurately, merely to keep various members of the audience happy as they bawled out responses to Rolf's repeated queries: 'Anybody here from Ireland? Scotland? America? Moldova? Tanzania?'

MICK GAFFEY

Mick Gaffey had been a professional drummer for nearly twenty years when he got a call from Bob Clifford, Rolf's publisher, to join Rolf's band. His first performances with Rolf were to promote 'Stairway to Heaven', and he witnessed the changes that Rolf's new-found student celebrity status necessitated.

When I joined The Roo Brothers, as Rolf's band is affectionately known, we had a rehearsal at Wigmore Hall, which was fantastic, and went straight on to do TV shows like *The Word* and *Top of the Pops*. We then progressed to our first live performances. Rolf's set was very different in those days; it was essentially the show he had been performing on the cabaret circuit for many years. We would open with 'Tie Me Kangaroo Down, Sport', and carry on with the song for quite a while. There were at least six different arrangements of 'Kangaroo', including a country version, a Russian one with the accordion and several versions in different languages. Rolf had a routine in which he

would explain how many languages it had been translated into; then he would sing them all. So we'd be a good halfway through the show before we hit a song that didn't involve tying a kangaroo down!

Rolf's set has progressed considerably since then; it's more interesting rhythmically and there's a lot of variety in the songs. In many ways, Rolf is actually a percussionist. He has a very keen sense of rhythm and cross-rhythms. He uses breathing techniques, Ee-fin' and Eye-fin', in a very percussive way, and his Aboriginal clap sticks and Jew's harp playing is superb. His wobble-board, of course, is his own invention and trademark. He told me once how he came to discover it. He had painted the background for a picture of the magician Robert Harbin on a board, and had left it on an oil heater to dry. When he picked it up to see if it was ready, it burnt his fingers. Rolf was worried the board was going to go up in flames, so he propped it between his palms and shook it to cool it down. The board wobbled, and the sound and rhythm it produced immediately struck Rolf. It was definitely a eureka moment for him, and he simply incorporated it into his act. Robert Harbin never got his portrait, because Rolf used it as his very first wobble-board. Nowadays he travels with custom-made wobble-boards which he creates and paints at home with his own individual designs.

Rolf is very particular about the sound and feel of his wobble-board, so on-stage he goes through a ritual of tuning it up. He bends and pulls it quite violently until he gets the right reaction and sound from it. He has actually snapped a few wobble-boards whilst doing this. The audience thought it was part of the act, but he was mortified!

That's not the only time Rolf has been mortified on stage while the audience laughed, blissfully unaware that things had gone badly awry. Before a gig in Grimsby recently he asked if anyone in the dressing room had a safety pin; his orange Jake the Peg trousers had been returned from the dry-cleaners *sans* the clip. As no-one had a safety pin, he borrowed a lace from Alan Dunn's trainers, which he used to tie the trousers up. When he performed the song on stage things were going fine until about the second verse, when all of a sudden his strides started falling down! Because he uses one hand to operate his extra leg

– diddle diddle diddle dum – Rolf was unable to pull them up himself. Hughey Hughes, Rolf's factotum, was motionless at the side of the stage. Suddenly he reared up like a horse, rushed on to try to raise them up again, but to no avail. At the end of the song, Rolf looked out at the audience, who numbered about 2,000 people, and said, 'Is there any chance that we can keep this just between me and you?'

It's great to work with someone who is so genuinely popular and successful. It's nice to be part of his 'bubble', and the songs are great fun to play. Everywhere we go Rolf is loved, we're very well looked after and the food is always gorgeous. In the early days we used to have pizza before the show and then go on stage feeling a little bloated and sick. Now we tend to have a curry before we play. We still end up feeling bloated and sick, but it's a better class of bloated and sick than we felt with the pizzas!

ALAN DUNN

Alan Dunn has been Rolf's keyboard and accordion player since the release of 'Stairway to Heaven'. In addition to working with Rolf, Alan is also a member of Bob Geldof's band.

On *The Word*, the first TV show we performed with Rolf, we had to hang around for ages between the camera rehearsal and the actual show. After a long, impromptu musical jamming session with Rolf in the band's dressing room – singing, banging, and playing the accordion, stand-up bass, guitar etc. – the entourage transferred next door to Rolf's dressing room, where the refreshments were! While chatting away I noticed Rolf kept looking at me from the other side of the room. I didn't know him that well then, and felt a little self-conscious about his attention, but a while later he produced a brilliant sketch of me. He said that he'd found my face an interesting shape, so had drawn it on hotel writing paper. I wish I'd known he was drawing

me, I'd have kept my head still – in the picture, one ear seems a little lower than the other! Rolf's a fantastic artist, but if you ever find yourself sitting for him, don't move around too much!

Rolf designed his accordions himself, and had them made in Italy by Scandalli, the then Rolls-Royce of accordion makers. I love his accordion playing; he has a very strong approach. When he performed in the early days of his career, the accordion was all he had to accompany his singing and with it he can go on for hours, as we witnessed at *The Word*.

Wherever we play Rolf will include local regional songs in the set. He knows many from Scotland, Ireland, America, his parents' homeland of Wales and various parts of England, but I was amazed that, while playing for the East London University, where there are lots of Asian students, he proceeded to exhibit his Indian repertoire! The song he sang was in Hindi and called 'Meera Juta Hai Japani'. I think the gist of the song is something along the lines of, 'My shoes are Italian, my trousers are from America, my scarf is English, my watch is Swiss etc., etc., but my heart is from India.' Rolf had done some work in India many years earlier and had asked one of his hosts for the most popular Indian song of the day and had learned it. I've no idea how he remembered it after such a long time, but his solo rendition that night, in the original language, sent the audience absolutely wild.

RICK BOLTON

Rick Bolton has performed with Rolf on only a handful of occasions. But, with his tongue wedged firmly in his cheek, he remembers them very clearly!

I can remember listening to Rolf Harris as far back as the early Sixties. I have a vivid memory of seeing 'Jake the Peg' on *Top of the Pops* and, of course, 'Two Little Boys', which I have to admit I never really liked. Despite this, I felt honoured to be asked to deputize for Graeme, Rolf's regular guitarist. Rolf is probably the most famous person I've ever worked with, so that in itself is a beautiful thing! Generally, I've enjoyed playing with Rolf very much, although it's been more difficult than I had anticipated. There are funny little corners in Rolf's arrangements that can trip you up when you least expect it. About half of Rolf's material involves the use of only three chords, but they're often the hardest things to get right. If you put one of the three chords in the wrong place, it inevitably sounds terrible. As Rolf's band are all such consummate musicians, that can be a little embarrassing.

I have thoroughly enjoyed performing at the large-scale events Rolf plays. The most memorable show was an outdoor concert to about 15,000 people in South Shields. At one point in the show, the band, unbeknown to Rolf, who was chatting away at the front of the stage, all donned false beards and glasses, becoming instant Rolf lookalikes! Apart from me, that is. I did my best, but I have very little hair on my head; well, I have to be honest, I have none. The audience started to laugh, and when Rolf looked round he was highly amused by the whole scene. However, he noticed that I didn't have enough hair to make the illusion complete, so he asked the man on the merchandising stand to bring some more false beards on stage. These were then pasted onto my scalp, and transformed themselves into a Rolf wig.

At the same show a dog started barking in the audience. Rolf began to perform his inimitable dog impression and the dog looked up. He was probably terrified, because Rolf's barking coming through the amplified sounds of the speakers would have sounded like a giant dog barking back at him. The howling between man and beast went on for ages, and only stopped when the embarrassed owner led the dog away!

It has always been fun working with Rolf. And now, of course, I love 'Two Little Boys'!

MICHAEL EAVIS

Michael Eavis has run the Glastonbury Festival for over twenty years on his land at Worthy Farm. During that time it has become the biggest and most influential of all the summer music festivals in Britain. It was in 1993 that Rolf made his triumphant début at the festival.

Before we booked Rolf for Glastonbury we had a discussion as to whether he would be suitable or not. At the time we thought his audience was slightly different to ours, so it was a little risky, but we decided it was a risk worth taking in the light of his recent success with 'Stairway to Heaven'. On the afternoon he was due to appear I made a point of going down to the mixing desk with my wife, Jean. We were amazed to see so many people there to watch Rolf. There were tens of thousands of people waiting for him, and more pouring in, which was fantastic. When I've taken what I consider risks in previous years sometimes it hasn't worked out. To see that many people there to see him was absolutely incredible. Once he came on and ventured to the front of the stage, he received a rapturous welcome, like a huge pop star, and when he started his songs, everybody knew the words and they were all singing along. It was extraordinary. They had obviously been weaned on Rolf Harris when they were children; they'd played his records and they had stayed with them. Rolf was evidently part of their growing up and, even though many of them had aged, they still remembered the lovely pure childhood they'd once had.

Afterwards Rolf kindly came and played at my sixtieth birthday party. It was a surprise party. I didn't know anything about it, and I don't really know how Jean persuaded him to come, but he was great. Rolf is a star performer; he is very flexible and can fit into almost any event. We had him back in the acoustic tent in 1998, and it was full to bursting. Rolf has been great at Glastonbury; he creates a fantastic atmosphere, and hopefully we'll have him back again soon!

5

INSTRUMENTS OF TORTURE

Through the years Rolf's name has become synonymous with a host of different musical instruments and sounds. When you hear a didgeridoo you think of Rolf Harris. A Stylophone . . . Rolf Harris. Heavy-breathing rhythms . . . Rolf Harris again. The wobble-board . . . that's Rolf Harris, too. While it is only the wobble-board that Rolf can claim to have invented himself, his association with all of them is such that, to many people, he *did* create them. The instruments themselves range from among the oldest known to mankind to the very newest technology. The didgeridoo goes back to the dawn of time for the Aborigines, and in 1967 the Stylophone was the latest musical keyboard, a forerunner to the synthesizers and sequencers that came to revolutionize music and music making. As always, Rolf had his finger on the pulse.

BURT COLEMAN

During his career Rolf has been associated with a number of instruments from a wide range of cultural origins. But Rolf's involvement with the Stylophone, 'the world's smallest organ' as David Frost put it, would never have come about if it weren't for the determination of Burt Coleman.

In 1967 I was a partner in a company called Dübreq. We worked in the movie business, dubbing films and doing our own recording in a studio in Cricklewood. We had a small workshop in the basement of an ordinary shop, and that is where the Stylophone was born. It was actually invented by a man named Brian Jarvis, who was my partner, along with my brother. The original Stylophone was a hand-made model fashioned from an old transistor radio case, but the system was there: a stylus on a circuit board, which was coated with nickel to prevent it from being scratched. Once Brian had invented it, my job was to get it on the market. I visited all the big musical-instrument makers and dealers, and they loved it, but felt it was a toy. When I went to a toy company, they said it was a fantastic idea, but that it wasn't a toy, it was a musical instrument. I came across this problem all the time, and simply couldn't get anyone to promote it or take it on.

I realized that I had to get a name behind the Stylophone, and the obvious name at the time was Rolf Harris; not only was he riding the crest of a wave, he was evidently a very charming guy – and still is, of course! I knew he would love the product, so I wrote to his agent, but didn't get a reply.

About a month later I saw Rolf's picture on the cover of the *Radio Times*. I phoned up the BBC and found out where he was rehearsing for his new show, jumped in my car and raced down there. When I arrived, I walked past the doorman into the studio, where Rolf was having a cup of coffee with one of his guest stars, Georgia Brown. I walked straight up to him, apologized for interrupting and shoved the Stylophone into his hands. I showed him how it was played, then he looked at me and said, 'That looks good, but you're a cheeky bugger for walking in here!' Fortunately, though, he loved the product and wouldn't let it go. I asked whether it would be possible for him to play it on his show, but he said that would have to be the decision of his producer, Stewart Morris, who was away with the flu.

It felt like a brush-off, so I returned dejectedly to my two partners and told them it wasn't going to happen. Then, out of the blue, I received a phone call from Rolf. He said, 'It's Rolf here. Stewart's back, and I'd like you to bring that thing along so we can have a chat about it.' I immediately raced straight down to the studio. Stewart not only liked the Stylophone, he thought it was excellent, and it was obvious that Rolf did, too. He asked me if it had been on television before, so I told them it hadn't, but that it was going to be on the Frost programme on ITV, just to give them a bit of a push. In fact, I had been scheduled to appear on the Frost show with the Stylophone several weeks earlier, but had been scrapped at the last minute owing to an unscripted fight that had erupted on-screen between union leader Clive Jenkins and one of his disgruntled members. Anyway, Stewart said, 'Don't give it to Frost, give it to us and we'll put it on for three Saturdays in a row, peak viewing time, eight o'clock on a Saturday night.' I couldn't believe it because Rolf Harris was *the* star of the moment, and his show had millions of viewers each weekend.

I gave Rolf the Stylophone, and the first Saturday night he introduced it as a new British invention. He said, '1930 was a good year for music because the electric organ was invented and I was born! And this week a British company has come up with this.' He held the Stylophone up in front of the camera. He'd rehearsed with a thirty-piece string orchestra and played the first eight bars of 'Moon River', then the orchestra came in. It was fantastic. Rolf got a tremendous ovation; the audience wouldn't stop clapping. He then announced that the following week they would have the Young Generation playing Stylophones, but at that stage we hadn't made any others, so we worked frantically all week to produce six more and they played Paul McCartney's 'Yesterday', with Rolf taking the lead. Again, it was superbly done.

The final week was with Marco Segnore, a renowned Italian accordion player. I actually sent a Stylophone to him in Italy for him to practise on. Rolf and Marco did an accordion duet, and then Rolf pretended to show him a Stylophone for the first time and Marco played the sabre dance. From then on our phone never stopped ringing, and over the next few years we sold about four million Stylophones worldwide. But much of its success was down to Rolf and the people he introduced it to on television. Nobody could have done what he did; he even played a duet with Liberace!

We held a party for the millionth Stylophone we manufactured. Rolf was guest of honour, and he did an act, which was fantastic. The thing about Rolf is he's the sort of chap you can talk to, and the sort of chap who will listen to you. He's not a big head; he's simply a nice person. I love him to bits, that fella!

DANA GILLESPIE

Dana Gillespie has worked successfully for many years in the fields of contemporary jazz and blues. Never afraid to push the boundaries of music, Dana first met Rolf when she was recording her own version of 'Sun Arise'.

Rolf and I share the same birthday, along with Eric Clapton, Johnny Walker and my piano player, Dino Baptiste, whom Rolf has also worked with. Of course, I'm not seventy, but there are certain similarities between us, and in some areas we are like soul mates.

I originally got to know Rolf in 1992 when he came to record on my album *Methods of Release*. He joined us on that particular album because I had wanted to do a version of 'Sun Arise'. I'd gone to the publishers to ask permission, and they had suggested I ask Rolf to perform the didgeridoo part. It had never occurred to me that he might be free, available or willing. When he turned up at the studios he informed us he could only stay for half an hour. In the event he stayed for five, which I now know is very typical of Rolf. When he gets into something, he gets involved and finds it impossible to swan in and out. Rolf becomes part of whatever he's doing, which is one of his charms, and in the end he performed on a number of other tracks on my album.

We asked him to perform his vocal noises – his Ee-fin' and Eye-fin' – on a very fast dance track that had an Indian feel to it. The studio was filled with musicians who were working on the album, including the drummer from Simple Minds and two players from Pink Floyd. We thought we would only get about twelve bars from Rolf, but he went into the vocal booth and did seven minutes' worth of vocal noises. When he came out we all got down on our knees and bowed to the great master of the sound. I've always admired people who can make an instrument from their own mouth, like the Mills Brothers, who did it so successfully in the Fifties. To me Rolf is the same calibre. I have never come across anyone else who can do it like him. We call it 'Some Enchanted Ee-fin'!' I know most people think of Rolf as either the *Animal Hospital* presenter or singer of humorous songs like 'Tie Me Kangaroo Down, Sport', but for things like Ee-fin' and playing didgeridoo he truly is a fabulous musician. He's great for body instruments, too, and on another track we had him hitting his chest and legs rhythmically, which sounded wonderful. I have great respect for percussion players and, essentially, that's what Rolf is.

Shortly after we had finished making that album there was a benefit concert at the Hammersmith Odeon. It was for an old friend of mine, Mick Ronson, who had died of cancer. I invited Rolf to the show, which was attended by many rock luminaries, including members of the Stones. Everyone performing had worked with Mick at some time or other, with the exception of Rolf, but when I introduced him on stage to play the wobble-board during our set, the audience went wild for him. I've since been to his gigs and have seen the audience go completely berserk for him. There's a kind of magic to Rolf that's different from any other performer.

Rolf has now appeared on the last eight albums I've recorded. Anyone who doesn't take Rolf Harris seriously as a musician has got him completely wrong. They are seeing only the outer surface of the man, but there is so much more to him than simply Rolf the personality. Two years ago he came out to Mustique, where I run a blues festival every year. He joined us on stage and played some boogie-woogie piano. He's quite at home with blues players; they treat him as a fellow musician.

We have become great friends during the last few years and, as well as coming to Mustique, he and Alwen have stayed with me in Italy and we have travelled to India together. That was an amazing trip. I had told Rolf it was to be a music-free visit, but after three days he was suffering from didgeridoo withdrawal symptoms! He found a piece of plastic tubing in a builder's yard, and immediately got back didging as normal, much to the joy of everyone.

SHINING BEAR

Shining Bear is one of the world's leading exponents of the didgeridoo. He started appearing with Rolf in 1997, joining his band after an impromptu performance at a charity dinner, and since then he has formed a close friendship with the Harris family.

Rolf is the man who first inspired me with the sound of the didgeridoo. He is also the man who, as a child, I genuinely believed had three legs. My mother recalls, to this day, that I could not get it into my head that Jake the Peg was an act.

In 1997 I was invited to a photographic exhibition to play the didgeridoo. It was a fund-raising function for Holly Lodge, a day-care centre for autistic kids and young adults with severe challenges. I was kneeling on the floor, talking to a group of people about the kooka-burra and what it represents for the Aborigines in Australia. I pointed the didg at the door and started to create the sounds of the kookaburra. As I was playing, Rolf and Alwen Harris walked through the door. Rolf froze on the spot and stayed there until I'd finished. He came over and told me that all the hairs on the back of his neck had stood up and that he had never heard kookaburra played in such a way on the didgeridoo before.

I was a guest at the official dinner after the exhibition, and sat at Rolf's table with my didg. Rolf said, 'Do you fancy doing "Sun Arise" with me?' I couldn't believe it – being asked to perform with a man who I could only describe as an icon. If it hadn't been for Rolf the Western world may never have heard of the didgeridoo. Of course I fancied playing 'Sun Arise' with him!

Rolf has a very close friend named David Blanasi, an Aborigine who is a didgeridoo master. Rolf has toured Australia with David several times, performing with him at expos in Japan and the USA, and on stage at the Sydney Opera House. Before this, in 1969, he filmed a series in the north of Australia called *Rolf's Walkabout*, and David was his Aboriginal guide for a section of it. At the time it was a groundbreaking series that undoubtedly helped to break down some of the myths and barriers that existed between the Aborigines and the white Australians. When you look at that programme you can see the mutual acceptance and respect between Rolf and the Aborigine people. Rolf has a great regard for and comprehension of their issues; he under- stands how hard it is to live on the land as an indigenous population. He has a great awareness, and through his incredible ability to communicate in an open and honest way he has helped that awareness spread to others.

After my initial rendition of 'Sun Arise' with Rolf, he invited me to join his band. Since then I feel privileged to have become a close friend of both Rolf and Alwen. Alwen is an extraordinary woman, so full of joy and laughter, and one of the gentlest, most loving people I've met. She is Rolf's backbone and is totally unconditional with her love. Alwen Harris is definitely Rolf's best friend; nobody knows him like she does. And, like Rolf, she's a flamboyant one-off. She can light up a room simply by walking into it.

I've spent a lot of time with Rolf since joining the band and, on occasions, I've driven him to his shows. Rolf is a dreadful passenger; he's a control freak. It quickly becomes clear to anyone who drives Rolf that he likes to be driven in a certain way. If you don't drive that way he'll let you know about it very unceremoniously. I remember one of our first journeys, when I drove him all the way from London to Glasgow. Rolf slept for most of the way – the car is sometimes the only place he actually gets some rest! When we got to Glasgow, Rolf was just waking up, and we pulled over to ask someone the way to the venue.

'I don't know why you're asking me, mate. I'm from Perth, Australia,' he said. All the way to Glasgow and the first person we met was from Rolf's hometown! Rolf and he had a chat about Perth and we moved on. As we were driving around trying to find the venue, Rolf suddenly said, 'For goodness' sake, Bear, you're driving like a hairy goat.' I've since discovered that this is Rolf's phrase for people who, in his eyes, are driving badly; they become hairy goats. From that day onwards, before we start a journey, I look at him and say, 'There will be no hairy goatishness on this journey!' That always brings a great smile to his face, but it doesn't always work.

On the rare occasions that Rolf relaxes he likes to carve wood. He made a wonderful seat from an old tree stump; it had a great big foot with a toe sticking up on one side and another foot on the other. When you sit on it, it looks as if you're sitting on half a pair of legs. He made Bindi an amazing toilet-roll holder with a head carved on the end of it from an old piece of beechwood he found. He also makes chain links with wood, carving the wood so that there's no break in it. I think this pastime acts as an inner focus for Rolf, taking him to a really calm place. Rolf's spirituality is very personal to him. He has a great faith in the divine, and an amazingly open heart. I've never once heard Rolf raise his voice. He's an incredibly gentle man, not just a gentleman.

KATE BUSH

Kate Bush has been one of Britain's most successful solo artists for over twenty years. When Kate was recording her 1983 album, The Dreaming, *she invited Rolf to perform on one of the tracks.*

I've always been an admirer of Rolf's. I remember watching his programmes as a child, when he used to create his fantastic paintings. No-one could tell what the picture was going to be until the very last minute. I found the way he could hold people's attention absolutely fascinating. It was only ever at the very last dab of paint that suddenly the lines and blots became a recognizable picture.

I was a big fan of Rolf's music as well as his painting, particularly of the song 'Sun Arise'. When I was making my fourth album, *The Dreaming*, I'd written a track about the Aborigines. I needed a really good didgeridoo player for the song, and I immediately thought of Rolf. He is an excellent musician, particularly when it comes to the didgeridoo, and Rolf is incredibly knowledgeable about music. He was so nice when he came to the studio. We spent a day together working on the track, and he really is an adorable man. It was a fun day, as well as being interesting, and music is so exciting when it's fun as well as productive. I got exactly what I wanted from the didgeridoo; Rolf created the perfect atmosphere for the song. I hope very much to work with him again one day.

It was a real thrill for me to meet Rolf, especially as I had been a fan of his for so long. In a way, he was everything I wanted him to be and more. He is such a compassionate man, and that's why he presents *Animal Hospital* so well. I don't think anyone else could present that programme in the same way. Rolf is a true original.

PADDY BUSH

Paddy Bush is Kate's brother and works closely with his sister on her albums. A producer and respected authority on world music, Paddy was taught to play the didgeridoo by Rolf when he recorded on Kate's album The Dreaming. *But Paddy has far more than that to thank Rolf for . . .*

Rolf had an exceptional influence on me from a very early age, mainly because of 'Sun Arise', which was the first record I ever bought. I remember seeing a programme called *The Five O'Clock Club* in the early Sixties; it was the show children watched when they came home from school. One week it featured Rolf, and he painted his own back-drop while telling a story, in effect creating his own stage and his own scenery, then he took out his didgeridoo and started playing 'Sun Arise'. I had never heard anything like it. I phoned the TV station to get the details, and went out to buy the single the next day.

Rolf's early use of the didgeridoo unveils an aspect of Rolf that many people have never picked up on. Nowadays the Western world is used to the phenomenon of world music, and we hear sounds from other cultures quite regularly in our own pop music. Before it was called world music it was called ethnic music and was listened to pre-dominantly by musicology students. Before it was called ethnic music it had no name, and it was then that Rolf experimented with it, long before anyone else. Most people don't realize that Rolf was not only right there at the beginning of the world-music phenomenon, he possibly initiated it. The wonderful thing about Rolf is that he doesn't see any barrier or frontier when it comes to music. It doesn't matter where a tune comes from, if he likes it, he'll do something with it. With 'Sun Arise', he heard an Aboriginal song he liked and simply added some English words.

Throughout his career, Rolf has performed what I can only describe as unique experiments with his music. I think Rolf saw 'Sun Arise' as a unique experiment. If my memory serves me right, after 'Sun Arise' he recorded a song that very few people will remember called 'I Know a Man'. It was a multi-track recording, with two Rolfs singing on the song. It must have been done on one of the very early four-track tape recorders, enabling the music to be on two tracks and Rolf on the remaining two. Once again, Rolf was experimenting. Everything that Rolf has approached has this element of unique experimentation to it. That is why there's a big stylistic difference between 'Sun Arise' and 'Two Little Boys'. And 'Stairway to Heaven' was undoubtedly a unique experiment. His approach is brilliant; quite possibly inconsistent, but that is part of its brilliance.

It was an amazing experience when he did some recording with us on Kate's album *The Dreaming*. Although I was excited that we were going to have *the* Rolf Harris on a session, I was unsure of how he would be as a person, but he was so open and friendly. One of the things Kate likes to do when she is recording is give the musicians a free rein. She loves the idea of using a person and their talent, so she wanted Rolf to see what he could contribute to the track. He turned up at the studio, Abbey Road, with a whole arsenal of didgeridoos, including a telescopic one that could be tuned to any pitch. The expressions on the faces of the sound engineers when they heard the sound of the didgeridoo coming back in the control room was incredible – a look of absolute amazement. I can remember someone asking, 'What's inside it? What's making that noise? Is it some kind of reed mechanism?'

'No, no, it's just this,' Rolf said, and blew a raspberry.

On that day Rolf gave me my first didgeridoo lesson. I couldn't play it before that. Kate had been sent an instrument from Australia, which was basically a bit of old tree with a weird bend in it, and a hole you could almost get your head in. When I tried blowing on it my lips just disappeared inside the thing. It sounded like someone trying to clean a toilet! I showed it to Rolf and he said, 'No, no, no, have one of these.' He gave me my first proper didgeridoo, and showed me what to do with it. From then on, when we had him back for future sessions, he'd check me out for progress. The biggest credit I can give to Rolf for his teaching technique is that by the time we did Kate's next album, *Hounds of Love*, I was able to play didgeridoo well enough to perform on the song 'The Big Sky'. As Rolf remarked, 'I did myself out of a job there!'

I love Rolf. I think he's a fantastic, highly influential man. I've often said, if I could come back as anyone else at any time, I would come back as Rolf Harris in the 1960s, and I would paint my own scenery and background.

6

PHYSICIANS AND BEASTS

In August 1994 *Animal Hospital Live* was first screened on BBC TV. Since then there's been no looking back. In 1999 it won the coveted National Television Awards prize for Most Popular Factual Entertainment Show an incredible fourth time in five years. The show has enthralled animal lovers and captured the hearts of viewers from all generations and walks of life. According to Rolf, the stars of the show are the animals themselves, but everyone involved in the programme, both on and off the screen, agrees that Rolf is the magic ingredient that gives *Animal Hospital* its unique place in the hearts of the nation. As Tim Moses, one of the show's cameramen, puts it, casting Rolf in the role of chief presenter 'was a touch of genius.'

The person responsible for that genius was *Animal Hospital*'s original executive producer, Lorraine Heggessey.

LORRAINE HEGGESSEY

Lorraine Heggessey is currently Director of Programmes at the BBC. In 1994, the BBC Science Department had recently employed her as a freelance, where she was assigned the job of executive producer of a new programme, Animal Hospital. *Here she recounts how she came to pick Rolf Harris as presenter for the new show.*

When I started in the Science Department at the BBC, I was the first person to join from a general programming background, as opposed to being a science specialist. One of my first assignments was as executive producer for a new show, which was described to me as an animal version of *Hospital Watch*. I had a meeting with the team who were producing the show, and they explained to me that in the Science Department there was a tradition of hands-off executive producing. I looked at them and said, 'Well, I can tell you now that one thing I am *not* is a hands-off exec!'

At that stage they had decided on a female presenter, Lynda Bryans, but they hadn't chosen the man. In those days the fashion was to have everything presented by alternative comedians. I visited the Harmsworth Hospital with Fiona Holmes, who was the series producer, and I felt it was a very genuine place. The people who went there brought their pets for a reason: they cared about their animals. I realized we had to have a presenter who would be able to com- municate with ordinary people. Some celebrities can only talk to other celebrities; they may be very amusing company, and extremely capable when talking to media luvvies, but put them with a real person and they dry up! I also felt we couldn't have an alternative comedian up there because, frankly, it's not a funny subject.

It was also important that we had someone who cared about animals. I was trying to think laterally, because I've always enjoyed coming up with left-of-centre ideas. I had thought of various people, including Ken Livingstone, but for one reason or another nobody was quite right. One day, in desperation, I said to the researcher, 'Bring me a list of every celebrity associated with every animal charity.' There was a crowd in the office as I scanned down the list. I got halfway down, to the Cats Protection League, and there was Rolf Harris. I looked up at everybody and said, 'I've got it!'

Initially there was a lot of scepticism, but by this time I had really bonded with the team, particularly with Fiona Holmes and the other producer Sally Dixon, and everyone had accepted that I was going to be a hands-on executive. We arranged a business lunch with Jan Kennedy, Rolf's agent, and Rolf himself. He was having a low-key day when we met, and he certainly wasn't full of the sparkling repartee I've come to know and love, but he spoke quietly and gently, and expressed his feelings for animals in a genuine way. He didn't strike me as the kind of presenter who was going to set the world on fire. But I am quite stubborn, and by this time I had decided he was my man. Apart from anything else, I had seen him perform on television for years, so I wasn't going to judge him on one lunch. Though, apparently, Jan Kennedy gave him quite a talking-to afterwards!

But I did decide to check out one of his concerts. At that time he had just had a hit with 'Stairway To Heaven', and was developing a student cult following. I went to one of his gigs at a graduation ball at Portsmouth Polytechnic. The room was packed to the gunnels, and it was incredible to see an audience of students screaming along to his songs. When I was queuing up in the Ladies, I listened to the students talking. It was obvious that they really loved Rolf; he inspires genuine affection in people. I think that helped confirm for me that I was right in my judgement to have Rolf for the show.

I went back to the office and rang Alan Yentob, who at that time was Controller of BBC1. He was in the middle of a meeting, and I heard him shout out, 'Rolf Harris for *Animal Hospital*,' to the assembled crowd. He came back on the phone and said, 'No, he's got the thumbs down here!'

I said, 'I'm sorry, but I think he's the right person,' and he just said, 'Think again!'

The next day, Susan Spindler, who was acting head of the Science Department, had a meeting with Alan. She stopped by my office and said, 'Lorraine, who else are you prepared to offer?' I'm afraid I said, 'There is no alternative. Rolf is the only person I'm backing. If BBC1 wants to force me to take someone else, then I will, but I won't be held responsible for the consequences. If the programme is a disaster, on their heads be it!'

But the truth of the matter was that Rolf *was* a huge risk, because he had never done live work with an earpiece before. This was scheduled to be five days of live broadcasting, twice a day from the August Bank Holiday through to the Friday. In the end I got my way, as I normally do! We did a rehearsal on the Friday, which was a shambles for a variety of reasons, though fortunately not because of Rolf. When we went on air on the Monday the programme went quite well, and we had about six and a half million viewers. The Tuesday was similar, but on the Wednesday a rather tough-looking guy wearing a denim jacket came in with a very sick German Shepherd. Very sadly the dog had to be put down, and the man was utterly distressed. Rolf started crying as well, and he put his arm around the man, trying to comfort him. The emotion that came from Rolf was so genuine, and once we'd stopped filming Rolf took him off to his room. He sat there talking to him and consoling him for a good hour. That night, on national television, people saw the German Shepherd being put down and Rolf crying live on national TV. The next day it was the talking point of the nation. On Thursday night our ratings shot up to nearly ten million to equal *The Bill*, which was a first for any BBC programme. Alan Yentob rang me at the Harmsworth Hospital when I was in the production office, and the whole room went still. And he said to me, 'Lorraine. Rolf Harris – inspired choice!' And, to his credit, he will tell the story exactly the same way.

It was inspired, though in fairness, it could have been a disaster. Good creative decisions are usually risky ones. But in the long run, if it had been a disaster it wouldn't have been the end of the world. It would have been a week of live programming that could have done better. In the event, Rolf was a complete star. Rolf Harris and that programme were made for each other. We spawned a genre. It's hard to remember now, but the animal genre of programmes did not exist until *Animal Hospital*. There wasn't *Vets to Be* or *Vets in Practice*; no *Pet Rescue* or *Pet Heroes*. None of those programmes existed. Now, of course, the schedules are crawling with them. It won't be long before we see *Vets on the Loo*! But *Animal Hospital* was the first, and it's still the best!

TINA FLETCHER

Tina Fletcher has worked on the last two series of Animal Hospital. *As series producer, it's her job to talk Rolf through all the stories, and over the series she has built up a strong rapport with the* Animal Hospital *presenter. But she actually first met Rolf many years before.*

When I started on *Animal Hospital*, I mentioned to my mother that I was going to be producing the series. She said, 'Oh, he's so nice, that Rolf Harris. We all met him once!' She then recounted the time she had taken my two older sisters and me to one of his audience shows as children. Apparently Rolf had wandered over to us and said, 'What three lovely girls, I'm going to go and see if they're old enough to come on stage with me in the show.' Unfortunately, because I was only five and my sisters weren't much older, we were too young, but apparently Rolf was kind enough to come back and tell us himself.

Rolf and I had also met on another programme, when he had appeared in a studio show for me with his daughter, Bindi. The piece was looking at how she had become an artist and whether her father had influenced her decision to go into it as a career. On the day of filming it was my birthday, and as part of the interview Rolf did a sketch. At the end of the day Rolf gave me the picture. He had been told it was my birthday, so he'd signed the drawing and written 'Happy Birthday' on it. It was a really sweet gesture, but that's so typical of Rolf.

To work with, he is the best in his field. Rolf is so natural. I've worked with some celebrities who may seem fine for a few days, or even weeks, but after a while invariably another side of their character comes out. With Rolf, there is no other side. What you see is what you get and that's his charm.

We work long hours on *Animal Hospital*, and the days can be stressful at times. But Rolf, despite being the oldest member of the team, has an incredible energy which he transmits to everyone around him. When he walks into a room that energy is infectious; you can see people get picked up by it. He's exactly the same with the members of the public who appear on the show. Many people who agree to be filmed are quite shy, or at least they're not the type who would normally put themselves forward for such a situation. I believe they do it because they trust Rolf and know he's there for them. They see him as their ally, and he asks questions that he instinctively seems to know they would want asked.

When we select cases for the show, before we do any recording, the contributors come in and Rolf talks them through what is going to happen. He reassures them and, in a matter of half a minute, you can see them relax; you know that in that short space of time he has built up a trusting relationship with them. That applies to the animals as well; they're comfortable with him and he's comfortable with them. He is the only celebrity I've come across who has that uniqueness, that ability to make people forget he is a huge star. He never acts like one, and he never presumes that he is one.

That doesn't stop the animals from going for him, however. On one occasion I recall him being bitten and bleeding quite badly. His hand

swelled up, but he turned it into a joke. He went off camera, and when he came back he had a big plastic dog collar on and his hand bandaged up. He walked in, held his hand in the air and said, 'I'm ready to start again.' It was very comical, and even with a serious injury his sense of humour and fun never seem to leave him. I have the impression his family life is just as much fun. When I speak to him on the phone at home there's often bellowing laughter in the background, usually coming from Alwen!

Animal Hospital has been incredibly important to animal welfare. There is no doubt that public awareness of animal-health issues and problems has increased as a result of the programme. The show doesn't set out to be educational, but there is a drip-feeding effect that enables owners to look at their pets and recognize symptoms and ailments, and realize they may need treatment.

I believe Rolf is our magic ingredient in conveying that. He brought something to the series that you can't put your finger on and certainly could never have planned for. It's his natural manner and his ability to work with ordinary people. Rolf is a legend, yet he always has time for people; his genuine disposition comes across, and people believe in it. If I worked in television for another hundred years I don't think I'd ever work with someone I admire more.

RHODRI WILLIAMS

Although Rolf is the lynchpin to Animal Hospital, *he is not the sole presenter. Rhodri Williams has been co-presenting the show for two years, and is often out on location. Consequently, he had already done several shoots for the show before he actually met Rolf, a meeting he was looking forward to with a mixture of anticipation and apprehension.*

The first time I was due to meet Rolf was at the recording of the *Animal Hospital Roadshow* at the new aquarium in Plymouth. I'd been working on the programme for about two months before I finally met Rolf, and there had been a steady build-up of expectation. Every item I worked on, the directors and producers seemed to do nothing but talk about Rolf this and Rolf that!

I had hoped to meet Rolf at the hotel the night before filming, but he was late arriving and went straight to bed. Once it was evident I would have to wait until the following day and the actual recording I became even more nervous. I was particularly worried that I wouldn't have enough time to develop any rapport with Rolf. When I entered the restaurant the next morning I saw him having breakfast. He had his back to me, but it's impossible to miss Rolf; he fills a room. A little awe-struck, I walked over to his table. He looked up at me and simply said, 'There he is!' as if he'd known me all my life. I sat down and we talked all through breakfast, like old friends. Rolf put me at my ease immediately, and throughout the course of the day he made me feel very welcome.

That evening we went out for a meal. Everyone involved in the show was there, including the other presenter Shauna Lowry, the vets David Grant and Bairbre O'Malley, and the producers. I was the new boy and wanted to impress, so I'd decided not to speak unless I was spoken to – the usual protocol. But I'll never forget Rolf looking over the table at me with mischief in his eyes. 'Do you fancy a song?' he asked. I thought, Oh my Lord, what do I do?, with all the production team staring at me. 'Go on, a good Welsh song,' continued Rolf. I looked at him in disbelief, but he meant it. So I thought, Well, I'll do as I normally would, and that was it. I started singing with Rolf and away we went. That was on the day we met – a memorable day I'll never forget – and we've been singing ever since!

When I was at college in Cardiff in the 1980s, 'Two Little Boys' was our rugby-team anthem. We sang it as we drove down the M4 coming home from a match. It was part of the squad repertoire every Wednesday and Saturday. After I'd been working with Rolf for a while he asked me to do some backing vocals on his upcoming album. My immediate reaction was to panic, because I'm a little in awe of session musicians and singers like Rolf, who can listen to something once and perform it. When we recorded, I made a couple of mistakes, but they let me retake them. The experience was great fun, and now I can honestly claim to have sung on a Rolf Harris record.

Whilst Rolf's records are great, his live concerts are something else. They are like a one-man pantomime because he gets everyone involved. It's amazing to watch him capture an audience. The show has everything, from people wearing pretend beards and glasses to fans who genuinely love the songs and sing along. Rolf is so entertaining. It's a complete variety show going to watch him.

I'd already seen him perform live once in Perth, Australia, so when he asked me to a concert in London at the Swan in Stockwell, I was delighted. I was also a little apprehensive, however, because he'd said he would invite me on-stage to sing the two songs I'd recorded in the studio with him. When the time came to join him I was vaguely confident of my pitch and harmony line, but when the band started I couldn't hear a thing. There was so much screaming and shouting from the audience it was deafening. But it was a fantastic experience nevertheless; I'd never performed at a live gig before. I knew I was out of tune, but everyone was having such a great time that I thought, What the heck, I'll apologize later.

A few days after that I saw Rolf singing again, this time at the Rugby World Cup Final to a crowd of 72,500 and a global audience of millions. He has so much energy, which is why I loved him when I was growing up. Like most people of my generation, I used to love watching *Rolf's Cartoon Time* and seeing the characters develop. There was always a sense of anticipation: What's it going to be? Is it going to be my favourite cartoon? Is it going to be *Tom and Jerry*? Is it going to be *Woody Woodpecker*?

Another memory I have of Rolf from that time is his swimming advertisement, aimed at encouraging young people to learn to swim. In the commercial, Rolf comes up to the side of a pool and says, 'I was lucky!' He then recounts the story of how he fell in a river as a child and just managed to scramble to the side. In the advert he says something like, 'From that day on my mum said to me, "You gotta learn to swim!"' And then, at the end of the commercial, a bunch of kids come running after him shouting, 'Get him!' They all charge at Rolf and he gets pushed into the pool!

Rolf is never precious, and anything he asks for will be reasonable. I'll never forget when he did the *Animal Hospital Roadshow*. We were in the New Forest, and in most places where the show is filmed there are buildings, where a room is allocated for Rolf to rest in. This is affectionately known as Rolf's Room. In the New Forest we were in a big marquee, and behind the marquee was the production office and a two-man tent with a camp bed in it. I remember looking at it and asking, 'What's that?' only to be told, 'That's Rolf's Room!' I thought it was outrageous; he'd never get any peace in there. But he didn't moan or complain; he just went in, zipped up the door, had a lie-down and accepted that's the way it was. Rolf is so in touch with reality. He does the job very well, but he makes the most of everything and enjoys himself whatever the circumstances.

That's not to say he's unprofessional. Much of the time Rolf is a perfectionist. I was amazed, when I first met him, at how involved he wanted to be; he didn't want to be spoon-fed. He often has strong opinions about how things should be presented, but he's never pushy. Professionally, he is very switched-on, and he knows what he wants,

though he also has the ability to compromise. Life is all about compromise, in both one's personal and professional life, but many people don't see it like that. Rolf does, and I think that's the only way to have the longevity he's enjoyed.

The year I was born Rolf was hosting prime-time live TV – *The Rolf Harris Show* on a Saturday night. He was there when television really took off in the Sixties, and now, over thirty years later, he is still hosting prime-time TV. These days everybody knows Rolf Harris, whether they are aged eight or eighty-eight. Working on *Animal Hospital* we see everything, from children coming off a bus screaming, 'Waaaaah, it's Rolf!' to lovely old ladies saying, 'Hello, Mr Harris!' I find it inconceivable that Rolf is about to turn seventy. He still has the same energy, so he doesn't come across as an old star who has been around since the Fifties. He's the Peter Pan of show business; he hasn't changed and he hasn't grown up.

DAVID GRANT

In addition to the show's presenters there are other regular on-screen stars on Animal Hospital. *David Grant is head vet at the Harmsworth RSPCA Hospital where* Animal Hospital *was first filmed in 1994, and has participated in many of the shows. According to Lorraine Heggessey, David has a brilliant relationship with Rolf, and they have a lot of fun together.*

It's a strange feeling when you meet someone famous for the first time. You feel you know them well from the television, but to meet them in the flesh is quite a different matter. Personally, I get very starstruck, but with Rolf it was quite extraordinary, because he was very subdued when he first came to the Harmsworth Hospital. I expected him to come bouncing in singing 'Tie Me Kangaroo Down, Sport', but instead he came in quietly. He seemed slightly overwhelmed, probably because he had never seen so many animals and people running around in such a busy hospital before. It was quite an eye-opener for him. Also, he appeared to be evaluating the project, thinking things through, asking questions and wondering how he would cope with the show. At that stage he had no idea what he was letting himself in for, nor that *Animal Hospital* was going to take off in such a way. Nor, for that matter, did we!

Of course, once we actually started working on the programme it didn't take long for the true Rolf to blossom. He suddenly started singing and joking and enjoying himself. It was obvious that he'd found something for which he was eminently suited. All his entertainment and media experience over the years was brought into use, and from day three or four he was a changed man. You could almost see him thinking, This is good fun. I'm enjoying this!

Inevitably, we enjoyed it, too. And the great thing with Rolf is that he doesn't get in the way at all; he's actually quite helpful in the surgery. As far as I'm concerned, he's there to help me, so I make him hold the animals and grab their legs – whatever needs doing. We usually have a banter between ourselves, both on and off camera; he really is no different when we're not filming. I think that's the secret of great professionals like Rolf: their ability to be themselves on camera. Rolf can come across as though he's talking to a little old lady in her sitting room on a one-to-one basis. I remember him telling me once that, when he's looking at the camera, he thinks of himself as talking to one individual, not ten million people, and that genuinely comes across.

It is a part of what makes Rolf a true professional. He can listen to a director, to the owner of an animal and the vet, watch what's going on and still act as though none of it is happening. Behind his laid-back exterior is an extraordinarily hard-working and professional man who never seems to put his feet up. But he evidently enjoys it and never seems to be stressed. In fact, he gives the impression he's constantly relaxed, although in my view he works just a little bit too hard. I've often told him, 'For goodness' sake, Rolf, we've got another two months of this. Take it easy, put your feet up on Sunday.' But he never takes any notice of what I say!

We've had a million laughs since we started *Animal Hospital*, and that's largely down to Rolf. He is a very funny man, so it's a 'crack'; it's a joke a minute. I remember once having a parrot in the surgery. I don't know much about parrots, so I was trying to avoid having to do anything with it, and I certainly didn't intend performing an examination outside its cage. I was just about to wrap up the consultation when Rolf said, 'You gonna get him out of the cage, David?' I thought to myself, Thanks a lot, Rolf! but I couldn't back out of it, so I opened the cage door and the parrot hopped onto the owner's shoulders and started cackling with a long witch-like laugh. When I tried to examine him he took off after me and grabbed my thumb. I blame it squarely on Rolf!

Of course, there have been many sad times, too, and the emotional side of Rolf that is often seen on the show is a side of him we hadn't anticipated. We're fairly immune to it as vets. We see animals suffering every day, and what is regarded as shocking to many people is sadly quite normal for us. We had a kitten die in front of us – the runt of the litter whom the mother was neglecting. To me, it was simply nature taking its course, but Rolf was very upset by it. That incident struck me; I suddenly realized how hardened I am to it all. When you're a vet, doing your job day in, day out, it's easy to forget that the people who come to the hospital witness things they've never seen before. It can be quite a shock to their systems, and Rolf is very good at getting that emotion across to the viewers.

When Rolf works at *Animal Hospital* he is often under phenomenal pressure, so it's amazing to think that he's turning seventy. He looks fantastically young, and I think the reason he doesn't seem seventy is that he doesn't think like a seventy-year-old. He's obviously a spiritual man, and he has a great empathy with people, but he's not at all judgemental. In public, people flock around Rolf. Everyone wants to shake his hand, take a photo, get his autograph and just be with him. A bus came past us once, and it almost tipped over as all the passengers leaned out to see him! Rolf has tremendous charisma, and he has time for everybody. That, to me, is real star quality.

TESSA BAILEY

Tessa Bailey had been learning the didgeridoo before Rolf and the BBC team arrived in 1997 at the RSPCA Putney Animal Hospital, but Rolf helped her considerably with her technique. Here, she recalls enjoying Rolf's company from the word go, and confirms the importance of the show to animal welfare.

From the moment Rolf Harris came to Putney for the *Animal Hospital* show he was lovely. To put it simply, he was Rolf, the character he is on television, only in real life. He was funny, entertaining, yet at the same time very genuine. There was no playing the star; he just made friends with everyone in the hospital.

I had looked forward to the BBC's arrival with a mixture of anticipation and terror. I really didn't know what on earth it would involve, and everyone at Putney imagined it would be far more intrusive than it has turned out to be. In fact, in surgery it is quite a help, because we work at a slower pace. I'm used to working flat out. It's usually so busy that we only have time for five-minute consultations. It's quite difficult to slow down and take longer, which is what we have to do when we're filming, and that's quite a luxury.

It also took a little while to get used to the fact that Rolf has an earpiece which is linked to the producer, and that he has instructions which we don't know about coming down constantly. As a result, Rolf will suddenly ask a question or make a comment that seems to come out of the blue but is usually very pertinent. When I'm consulting alone I follow my own track of ideas and questions. But Rolf's presence actually makes it quite fun, and I've had to get used to being on the ball all the time!

I was learning the didgeridoo when the *Animal Hospital* team first arrived at Putney, but was struggling with my circular-breathing technique. By way of making conversation one day, I asked Rolf if he had any tips, and he was extremely helpful. I have a lot to thank Rolf for in that area, though my neighbours aren't so grateful!

Rolf has made such an enormous contribution to *Animal Hospital*'s success, and that, in turn, has helped many animals. Not only has it let people see the work of the RSPCA, it has also made people aware of what vets can do. It's great when people bring animals in and say, 'I saw this on the telly; I didn't realize you could cure it.' Or, 'We found this lump and now we know it may be serious.' We can now save lives because people have been made aware of their pets' serious problems. The vets and nurses are the experts on the veterinary side, the animals are the focus of attention, the TV crew do their work, but Rolf is the person who translates it all to the camera.

Rolf's most outstanding attribute, and the one that makes him so perfect for the role, is that he inspires trust. People *know* he's genuine, whether he's telling a joke, singing a song or being with an animal that's in awful distress. It's just sad for us when the series finishes; it feels like half the staff has gone. There's a week of mourning when they go because it seems so empty.

NOEL & TRUDY JONES

The animals and owners who appear on Animal Hospital *are real characters with genuine problems. When Noel and Trudy Jones came to the RSPCA hospital at Putney, they expected the worst for their cherished cat Tom. Meeting Rolf was the last thing on their minds, and they were initially reluctant to appear with him on the programme. Fortunately, their opposition to the idea was overcome, resulting in a happy ending for everyone involved, not least of all Tom.*

It was a bit of a surprise to find Rolf Harris in the building when we first arrived at the Putney animal hospital; it hadn't occurred to us that he might be there. But we didn't really think about it because, at that stage, our only concern was for Tom, our cat, whose leg was in a bad way. In fact, we were thinking that we should have him put down. We

certainly didn't want the vets to try to save the leg and cause Tom a lot of stress, only to have them come back to us and say, 'That was unsuccessful, now we'll have to amputate the leg.'

Originally, when they asked us if we would like our appointment with the vet filmed for the programme we said no, but in the end they talked us into it, and we're glad they did. Rolf was a very calming influence and very kind. We would have had a totally different outlook if he hadn't been there. It was Rolf who encouraged us to have Tom's leg pinned. We were going to say no, because we didn't want to see Tom with only three legs, and we knew that's what might happen if the pinning didn't work. Rather than put him through that misery, we thought it better to put him out of his misery. Rolf helped to influence our decision and we were persuaded to go ahead with the operation. If Rolf hadn't been there, there's no doubt that we wouldn't have gone through with it.

Rolf seems a genuinely good human being, not simply because he's famous but because he's good at lifting people's spirits. He also seemed to have a way with the cat. When we arrived, Tom was in pain and howling, but Rolf held and stroked him and seemed to calm him.

The vets did a wonderful job. Tom's leg has healed, and we're so pleased it's still intact!

7

WONDROUS CREATURES

In 1998, having just finished his seventh *Animal Hospital* series, Rolf embarked on a new show, *Rolf's Amazing World of Animals*. A natural progression from *Animal Hospital*, the show sets out to celebrate the relationship between humans and the rest of the animal kingdom. It deals with issues of environment, conservation and survival, as well as looking at some of the more incredible stories that come from the animal kingdom.

JOANNA LUMLEY

Joanna Lumley was a guest on Rolf's Amazing World of Animals, *championing a cause both she and Rolf feel very strongly about, Compassion in World Farming. However, their first encounter was a few years earlier at a Thames Television gala evening.*

I first met Rolf at Teddington Studios when he and I were guests on the same show. He came walking into the big make-up room at Thames Television, as it was then, in an electric-blue suit that seemed to be made of slub silk. There was something so excellent about that. It was at a time when everyone wore modest charcoal-grey or subtle, dull outfits, and Rolf came in like an electric eel. He's never grown up, and that's the truth of it. I think that's why he's got such an enduring place in people's hearts.

I can remember Rolf Harris from when I was eleven or twelve, and he had exactly the same voice and the same lunacy. But a lot of that off-the-cuff madness conceals a much deeper man. Like all people who are truly talented, which Rolf is, he quite often makes light of his talents and treats them as fun. Someone a little less talented than him would talk about their serious prowess as a musician or a painter. Rolf is a communicator, a broadcaster, and at every level he has succeeded, but because he makes light of it himself, it's easy for the world to think of him as a lightweight. But I learned long ago that there's nothing lightweight about entertainment.

Doing *Rolf's Amazing World of Animals* was my real getting-to-know-him time. We travelled on the train together, and spent all day freezing in a field on a lovely farm together. We are both passionately committed to animals and animal welfare, and this was a film about how the life of farm animals can be easily managed in an almost organic, free-range way, so that animals are properly treated. It's still the same business of rearing animals for meat or wool, but it's about doing it in a humane way, making sure they are comfortable, with good-sized stalls, sties and fields. The main point is to ensure that they are looked after properly, with no overcrowding, and that they are treated with respect and compassion, and to show that this can pay off in the end.

I was thrilled when I heard that we were going to be allowed to do a slot about this on Rolf's show. I was representing the organization Compassion in World Farming, which Rolf has helped on many occasions in the past, and Rolf's show was a wonderful opportunity for us to get the idea across. To my anxiety, at the moment we still have to pay so far over the market price for produce from kindly reared animals that only saints, or rather very rich saints, can afford to buy them. And having to rely on people's goodwill is not always the best thing to depend upon in a marketplace.

Rolf got the whole idea across very well. He has a huge humanity about him, without being soppy, and he is immensely kind. Whenever he's near creatures, children, adults or indeed any living thing, there's something buoyant and optimistic about him. He radiates a feeling that you can make a change and that it's worth doing.

As a child, I was a great fan of Rolf's music. We didn't have a television set as youngsters, so we played the gramophone a lot, and 'Tie Me Kangaroo Down, Sport' was one of our favourites. I think I know every last pause and gulp. A song like 'Sun Arise', with the didgeridoo introduction, is strangely moving, as is 'Two Little Boys'. It doesn't matter if a few people think it's wet, because our country has such an affection for that song; it has an amazing message for peace.

When I heard Rolf talking about that particular record on *Desert Island Discs*, it really moved me. I think a lot of people who have had something to do with war and warfare have a very soft spot for that song. He got a little choked up when he was talking about it, but I love him for that, and I love him for being himself. It's very easy to be cool and hip in this business, but it's very difficult to be an unchanged and blazing meteor.

JOHN CLEESE

John Cleese appeared on Rolf's Amazing World of Animals *in a programme filmed at Marwell Zoo, where John had carried out research for his film* Fierce Creatures. *As with many stars who have worked on Rolf's shows over the years, it wasn't John's first encounter with our antipodean hero.*

Prior to filming *Rolf's Amazing World of Animals*, I had already met Rolf on holiday, many years before on the island of Hydros. I'll never forget it, because we went snorkelling together, and he introduced me to the amazing breakthrough idea of snorkelling in a T-shirt to avoid getting sunburnt! I remember this being a fantastic revelation to me and my English friends, but, of course, for an Aussie it was an obvious trick. We spent some time together then, and I found him very entertaining company.

When I got the invitation to do the *Amazing World of Animals* programme, I was delighted to participate, not only because it was to be done at Marwell, which had helped me so much with information on how zoos work when we were preparing *Fierce Creatures*, but because I knew I would be comfortable with Rolf. It proved to be a very easy day's filming because he is so easy to work with. Not only does he know how to do the job, there's no ego with Rolf. You end up chatting very naturally, and that is always easy when you're talking about a subject that's interesting.

For both Rolf and myself, animal conservation is just such a subject. Many years ago, I visited the Gerald Durrell Zoo in Jersey. We were on the island shooting and Gerald, whom I only knew from his books at the time, sent us an invitation. He took us round the zoo, and during the course of our visit I was looking at a bird – the white-eared pheasant from China. One of Gerald's assistants told me the bird would be extinct if Gerald hadn't set about saving it, and it astounded me that one individual could do something as worthwhile as save a species.

Since then I have been involved in various conservation activities at different times, including a documentary about releasing lemurs that had been bred in captivity in Madagascar into the wild. The programme was well received and I enjoyed doing it, so working with Rolf on his show was a continuation of that. We actually went into the lemur enclosure at Marwell for the filming, which was great fun. They are the most delightful little creatures, though they are slightly mischievous. Once they have got used to human beings they are very tame. They will take food from you with such delicacy that you never feel they might bite you by mistake. They are very well-mannered creatures, although not awfully bright.

The same cannot be said for Rolf. As a performer, it is quite remarkable how many things he can turn his hand to with discernible dexterity. The media are not always willing to accept stars who, as Michael Palin put it, 'try to come out of their box'. It is almost as if they are offended by entertainers attempting to do something different. But with Rolf that doesn't apply, because he has always been recognized for his many different skills. I have always enjoyed him as a performer, but I particularly delight in the fact that one day he's sketching and the next he's doing a splendid song like the one about the brothers who grow into soldiers, 'Two Little Boys'. As for Jake the Peg, it's the most wonderful Vaudeville routine. Quite brilliant. I could watch him perform that once a week and never tire of it.

MICHAELA STRACHAN

Michaela Strachan currently presents her own animal programme, The Really Wild Show, *the long-running Children's BBC wildlife series. Michaela travelled to the north of Scotland with Rolf to do an* Amazing World of Animals *special on the dolphins of Moray Firth.*

I was six or seven years old, and one of my favourite possessions was a Rolf Harris album, which I thought were just fantastic. It was the first album I ever owned, and on it were 'Two Little Boys' and 'Tie Me Kangaroo Down, Sport'. I loved it; it was real singalong time when I played it, and I was a huge fan of Rolf's.

Consequently, when I was a guest on *Rolf's Cartoon Club*, I have to admit I was quite excited to be appearing alongside *the* Rolf Harris. After that, Rolf was a guest of mine on *The Wide Awake Club*. It's strange, but when I was presenting the Saturday morning show, I interviewed so many people that it was rare to have a guest on who would impress me. Many pop bands come and go, and singers are the in thing for about a year and then they return to obscurity, and often you don't really know who they are anyway! But Rolf is timeless; always there. A friend once told me what they thought was the secret to his success: basically, that he is Australian and therefore classless, so nobody brackets or labels him.

Mind you, I think his talents probably help a lot, too! These days, there is a lack of entertainers like Rolf who can perform in a variety of ways. There's almost no end to what Rolf can do, although he's very unassuming about his talents, and that, for me, is a large part of his charm. Rolf is also incredibly good at dealing with people; he really interacts with the general public. I travelled with Rolf to the Moray Firth in Scotland, where I've adopted a dolphin, for his *Amazing World of Animals* show. He has so much energy, which he gives unreservedly to complete strangers. We were on a boat full of children, and immediately Rolf began singing songs, playing the didgeridoo on an old bit of tube and signing autographs. He told me that he now gets quite tired by the afternoon, and I laughed and said, 'I'm not surprised, Rolf; maybe pacing yourself might be a good idea now and again,' because he just gives, gives, gives all the time. He entertained the kids constantly; I wish I had the ability to remember songs the way he does. His memory for words is incredible. He sang 'Flower of Scotland' with the children, and he knew more of the words than they did!

Rolf not only possesses charm, he is quite charmed! The day we went out onto the Moray Firth to film for Rolf's show it was a lovely day, and we were surrounded by dolphins within ten minutes. They skipped about the boat and the camera crew took some beautiful shots of them. Since then I've revisited the area for *The Really Wild Show*. On that occasion there was a force-eight gale, the boat was heaving – as were the crew – and we were lucky to see one dolphin!

When we filmed Rolf's show we were accompanied by a man from WDCS, the Whale and Dolphin Conservation Society. After we disembarked we went to a café, where Rolf kept the entertainment going and had us all singing. When Rolf went to the toilet the WDCS representative leaned over to me and said, 'If he wasn't well known, he'd be quite mad, wouldn't he?' And I suppose, in a way, he was right. You can get away with being eccentric when you're recognized from the television. Not many people can burst into song in a Scottish café without attracting unfavourable attention. I think that's probably why Rolf gets a kick out of being on TV; it means he can get away with doing whatever he wants, wherever he wants and whenever he wants!

DALE TEMPLAR

Dale Templar is a series producer for the BBC Science Department. Originating in BBC News and Current Affairs –'a rather serious background', as Dale puts it – she transferred departments in 1997 to join Rolf on the new Rolf's Amazing World of Animals *series. Since that time she has enjoyed many fun moments with Rolf, both in the studio and out on location.*

The most comical incident that has occurred with Rolf since we started on *Rolf's Amazing World of Animals* happened on the set. We were approaching the end of studio recording time, which is always a slightly tense period, and we had two pygmy goats in the room. They had already appeared in the 'Animal Crackers' part of the show, in which animals belonging to members of the public are seen getting up to strange and unusual antics. The pygmy goats' foible was that they ate paper. So for the finale of the show we planned to have Rolf sitting down with *The Australian*, a broadsheet newspaper, and while he tried to deliver his closing lines, the goats would eat the newspaper.

Everything was going to plan except that, unbeknown to Rolf, while he was delivering some of his lines standing up, one of the goats had wandered off and relieved itself on the seat he was about to use. What was particularly marvellous was that, because we were in mid-record, nobody else had seen it either, so everyone carried on regardless. Rolf delivered his lines and went over to the seat. He sat down, spoke a little more, and then literally broke down in hysterics. 'You won't believe what's happened,' he said, as he stood up and turned around so the audience could see his trousers. 'I've just sat down in a pool of goat pee!' Everybody collapsed – from the camera-men to the technicians up in the gallery, there wasn't a dry eye in the house, and the audience were beside themselves. Bearing in mind that I've worked in television with a lot of people, have done numerous studio recordings and seen a multitude of funny things happen, I can honestly say that I have never been in a situation where absolutely everyone on the team collapsed. It was the funniest moment in making television that I have witnessed. The next day, Rolf told me that when he returned home that night he'd never known the dog be so desperately interested in his bottom!

There must be something about Rolf and goats, because another time we were doing a shoot in the children's section of London Zoo, where they have an array of goats. We had decided we wanted Rolf to be encircled by the animals when we were filming, so we rather foolishly gave him some feed. Rolf gallantly did his piece to camera while the goats leapt further and further into his bucket. They finally pushed poor Rolf over, and there he was on the floor, true genius that he is, carrying on with this piece to camera, covered in goats!

There have been many times working with Rolf when I have discovered how truly professional and dedicated he is. We went to Mauritius, the land of the extinct dodo, to make a film about a conservation programme that looks after its many rare birds. The day before filming I went to all the different locations to make sure everything was fine. One of the sequences involved going to the nesting site of the extremely rare Mauritian kestrel in order to tag the baby birds. The expert with me pointed to the site, which was across a field in a little wooded area. It all looked fine and I decided not to go to take a closer look because I didn't want to disturb the nestlings more than necessary.

When we turned up the next day I discovered the place was really boggy, and it wasn't just the home of the kestrel family, it was also home to thousands of mosquitoes. We had to film quite a long sequence while being eaten alive by insects through our clothes. Rolf was amazing; he had them all over his body, yet he carried on with his usual good humour.

The thing about Rolf is that everybody knows him and he is incredibly generous with people. Whenever I'm asked, 'What makes Rolf so special?' I say, 'He's everybody's favourite uncle!' He is completely multigenerational. I remember when I was first told I was going to work with Rolf, I went home and dug out my *Rolf Harris Christmas Annual* from something like 1968, and this year, for my daughter, I've got an *Animal Hospital* book. It is quite amazing to find somebody who's managed to have that much appeal over so many years. Rolf is so down to earth, but he also has a kind of magic about him; a Hans Christian Andersen storyteller side.

In the summer, Rolf came to a party at my house, and I never quite worked out who got the biggest kick out of it, the adults or the kids. He was just magical with everyone; it was lovely to see. There was a wonderful moment when Rolf and I got on the dance floor, and the DJ said, 'There's a guy on the dance floor who looks just like Rolf Harris.'

So Rolf went up to him and said, 'I am Rolf Harris!'

The DJ replied, 'You're not. You can't be,' as if he couldn't believe Rolf might be at a private party.

Rolf just said, 'Well, I've got to be somewhere!'

8

HISTORICAL FIGURES

Long before *Animal Hospital* and *Rolf's Cartoon Club* had ever been dreamed of, Rolf had hosted a wealth of different TV shows through the Fifties, Sixties, Seventies and Eighties. He worked as a presenter at the dawn of television with his first children's programmes, *Jigsaw*, *Whirligig* and *Hi There (Hi T)*, where he interacted with puppets and characters such as 'Fuzz' and 'Willoughby'. In 1966 he fronted *Hey Presto, It's Rolf* with the lovable koala Coojeebear and Seamus O'Sean the leprechaun, and in 1967 Rolf made the leap to mainstream adult television in the hugely successful *Rolf Harris Show* with the Young Generation. In the ensuing chapter, key figures from some of those productions share their memories.

STEWART MORRIS

Stewart Morris was the producer of The Rolf Harris Show, *Rolf's groundbreaking Saturday night programme with the Young Generation. Stewart was born on the same day, in the same year, as Rolf.*

I was employed in the Sixties by the Light Entertainment Department at BBC Television, and, having something of a music background, I was drawn to music-based shows. Rolf Harris had been a very successful host of children's programmes for some years, but the BBC wanted to move him into the heat of the kitchen: mainstream TV. I was sent for by the then head of light entertainment, Tom Sloane, who in some ways was my mentor. He said, 'Right, Morris, you are going to produce a series with Rolf Harris!' I went away in stark terror, because I couldn't imagine how Rolf Harris was going to entertain at 7.30 p.m. on a Saturday night to a mass audience who perceived him as a children's entertainer.

I therefore started with a negative problem, but I got an idea from a programme I had seen broadcast from Italy with a presenter called Rita Pavoni. She had employed a crowd of street kids for the show, who followed her around wherever she went, and sat and listened to her. I thought, I wonder if this is the bridge between Rolf as a children's presenter and as a mainstream adult entertainer? Pursuing the idea, I thought that if I could train a group of youngsters they could be more than just kids following him around; they could perform, sing and dance with Rolf, and they could be his audience on stage.

I was looking for a choreographer who could put such a show together, and Dougie Squires' name came up. I'd seen him working with the Black and White Minstrels and the Mitchell Singers; he was the best choreographer for large groups at that time. I approached him and he said yes, and that's how the Young Generation was born. We auditioned thousands – and I mean thousands – of young hopefuls to get thirty dancers – fifteen boys and fifteen girls. The group lasted for ten years and some very successful people evolved from it. Dougie also taught Rolf to dance, and Alyn Ainsworth, the show's musical director, who is sadly no longer alive, helped Rolf with the singing. We would often do five-part harmonies with the kids, and Rolf would be absolutely astounding. Alyn did some sterling work with Rolf.

The combination of Rolf with his many talents and the Young Generation seated around him in genuine enthralment made the show a tremendous success. In each programme we would create a special scene for a big number. For example, we would create Sherwood Forest for a Robin Hood sketch, or Paris for a song about Toulouse

Lautrec. We even once created a swimming pool in the studio. At first the Design Department said, 'Forget it; we'll never be able to drain it, let alone fill it in the time!' But in the end the fire brigade, who were brilliant, helped us to create it (and, eventually, to empty it).

On the painting side, at the time very few people realized how talented a painter Rolf was, and still is, of course. He had exhibited; he was startling at portraits, and could produce a really amazing piece of work in a very short time. We sometimes cheated and would tell him there were only two minutes left when in fact there were two and a half in order to speed him up. It was just stunning; he could use six-inch brushes with various pots of paint to create the most wonderful paintings. He has a quite extraordinary ability.

Rolf and I always got on well; we were good friends. He could listen to ideas, and he would also make his point. Rolf always stood up and said what he thought. But he was very easy to work with, whether in the studio or outdoors. When he had his big hit with 'Two Little Boys', we filmed him singing it out in the country at dawn one morning in the middle of winter. We were frozen stiff!

Most of the time Rolf was totally in control, but I remember a show when his mind went blank. He was presenting Shani Wallace, a big star in those days, and, as ever, the show was going out live. Whilst Rolf was introducing her and giving her a big build-up, I saw a look of terror come into his eyes. I realized what had happened: he had blanked and couldn't think of her name. He just said, 'Ladies and gentlemen,' and started to applaud. I quickly cued the orchestra and mixed away from him. I'll never forget that look of terror; it was brilliant.

I've always admired Rolf. I remember a lunch given by the Variety Club to celebrate his success in this country. He stood up and said, 'When I came here from Australia, I never thought it would take so long!' which I thought was glorious. When he came over he was full of, 'I'm going to be a star, and it's going to happen overnight!' He did become a star, but he worked very hard for it.

To this day he hasn't changed. Rolf is the same guy with no giant ego, and he still has time for everyone. There's nothing phoney about Rolf. There are a lot of stars around who would do well to have a fraction of his talent and humility.

Rolf and the Young Generation in full flight.

With young fans at the annual Bray celebrity cricket match.

Appearing as a guest with friend and entertainer Val Doonican. Dig the fab gear!

Can you tell what it is yet?

The number-one dressing
room, Plymouth, where
Rolf spent the entire run
of *Jack and the Beanstalk*
painting his mural of the
pantomime and its cast.

Spot the cheeky monkey. Rolf on the set of *Animal Hospital Goes West*. Aquarius/BBC

Can I tie you down, sport? *Rolf's Walkabout*, 1969.

Two little boys. With John Cleese at Marwell Zoo.

Three little lambs.
With Joanna Lumley and
friend, championing the
cause of Compassion in
World Farming.

Compassion in World Farming

Rhodri Williams,
David Grant and
Rolf discuss the
Animal Hospital
schedule outside
'Rolf's Room'. Zoë Jelley

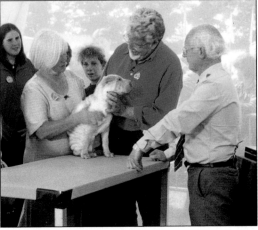

'Now if you could just say
"Aaah".' Rolf and guests on the
Animal Hospital roadshow.

Zoë Jelley

The Roo Brothers, 1998. Left to right, the band are: Alan Dunn, the book's editor Mark Walker, Graeme Taylor, Bernard O'Neill, Rolf, Shining Bear and Ray Weston. Hugh Hughes

The view from the stage during Rolf's triumphant set at Glastonbury in 1993. Mick Gaffey

Rolf's return to Glastonbury, 1998.
© Independent on Sunday/Tom Pilston

There's no place like home. Rolf and Alwen relax with Summer, Zuki and Rabbit.

DOUGIE SQUIRES

Throughout its successful run in the Seventies Dougie Squires was choreographer for The Rolf Harris Show. *Here he recalls the Young Generation's first meeting with Rolf and some of the subsequent escapades they enjoyed together.*

Thirty young, energetic and highly talented performers awaited the arrival of the star of the new BBC TV series they had been contracted to appear in. I was their choreographer and they had been christened the Young Generation by Tom Sloane, BBC controller at the time. I had chatted with the awaited star at a couple of production meetings, and he seemed a nice enough guy, but the YGs hadn't met him yet. If they were expecting a starry, sophisticated poseur surrounded by managers and yes men, they were to be disappointed, because this star was different.

The difference had turned him into a popular household name. He was unassuming, slightly eccentric, bearded, bespectacled, but most importantly, he was multi-talented. He stepped into the rehearsal room and our lives to face thirty pairs of eyes, along with mine and the all-seeing eye of our producer Stewart Morris. It had been Stewart's idea to combine the Young Generation with Rolf Harris, and from the beginning some sort of Saturday night TV history was created.

He was dressed in one of his signature bizarre, highly coloured sweaters, with an inevitable pair of pointed, battered, paint-splattered shoes! He also carried a good sense of humour, which never seemed to fail him. Only occasionally would the overpowering energy of thirty youthful, eager performers inspire a schoolmasterly show of impatience.

During the shows Rolf painted his extraordinary giant pictures surrounded by the YGs, who handed him buckets and brushes, each week wondering what vision he would come up with. He sang dozens of songs, and I took great delight in searching for material that suited Rolf's off-the-wall style for him and the kids to interpret. It was always a challenge to find original ways to choreograph and direct the strange songs that Rolf himself found from all sorts of ethnic sources.

In mini-musicals he played everyone from Henry VIII to Robin Hood, and he approached each character with a highly developed appetite for learning new things. He danced, too, sometimes with three legs, but always with the thirty young trained dancers. He often gave me the challenge of covering his wayward feet and legs to hide the fact that they didn't always do what he and I wanted them to.

Each week we would wonder what new strange musical instrument would come through the door with Rolf. A didgeridoo? An electric keyboard? Everything was a challenge to Rolf, and to us. During the years we filled the Saturday light entertainment slot, whether it was transmitted from Sweden, Germany or Shepherds Bush, we worked with all the top international stars. Rolf was never competitive and, in his own unique way, he held his own. He constantly proved that the show-business maxim, 'Never work with animals or children', doesn't apply to him.

I wish I could dish the dirt about this man, but there is none. Suffice it to say that this was a creative and entertaining period for us and the audiences, and Rolf was one of the giants of light entertainment. Thirty years later, he still is.

GEORGE CLAYDON

George Claydon played the role of Coojeebear in many of Rolf's children's shows in the Sixties and Seventies. Coojee was the mischievous koala bear that was always getting into trouble, and during their time working together, Rolf and George formed a unique partnership.

Playing the part of Coojeebear was a very special part of my life in the Sixties, not least because it was through Coojee that my wife and I got married. We had worked together in the early Fifties on a show; she was an acrobatic dancer and I was a comedian. When the show finished we went our separate ways and she married a Dane, had a little girl with him and then they split up. Her little girl, Lisa, used to watch the Friday night show *Hey Presto* with Rolf, and one particular evening Lisa was howling her head off. As my wife tells it now, she came in to see what her daughter was laughing at, and it was Rolf and Coojeebear. She looked at Coojee and thought, I wonder if that's Georgie Claydon in that skin? She wrote to the BBC to find out, and when it was confirmed she contacted me and we arranged to meet. From there we got married, and have been together ever since. I've always blamed Rolf for that!

When I started working as a koala bear with Rolf, I didn't have a name. In the first couple of weeks children were invited to send in ideas for a name and there was quite a big response. All sorts of weird suggestions came in, some of them quite indecent. We juggled the names around and Coojeebear came out as the favourite.

We used to base our routines on the concept that Rolf was my father and Coojeebear was a mischievous little child. I was naughty, but not nasty. So, for example, Rolf would give me a birthday present and I would unwrap it. I would get excited, but then I'd throw the present on the floor and start playing with the paper, dressing up in it or putting it on my head, and Rolf would get exasperated with me. Most of the sketches were based on things I'd seen children do. Very simple things, but as with most comedy, the simpler it is, the funnier it is. We would sometimes base the sketches on things Rolf's daughter, Bindi, or Lisa had done.

When we started we used to map out our routines, but after a few months we got so used to one another's characterization that we instinctively knew what we were going to do. I didn't wear the costume for rehearsals, and the director and assistants would watch us, fascinated that we didn't have any inhibitions about people being around; we simply got on with our characters. We didn't have a scriptwriter for our scenes; we used to make them up ourselves. I'm not absolutely sure how, we just seemed to have some kind of magic between us.

In 1974 Rolf went to the World Fair in America, representing Australia. I went with him because Coojeebear was appearing with Rolf in a huge symphonic work with an orchestra, slides and Rolf as the presenter. It was called 'Coojeebear and the Monster', and was performed at a huge concert in Knoxville, Tennessee. Rolf stood out as having so much talent. He did everything: blew his didgeridoo, painted a picture, sang, told jokes, played his accordion and did his unique breathing noises. In fact, on the strength of his performance I believe a country and western producer invited him up to Nashville. He'd never heard anything like it before, and probably never has since.

9

COURT JESTERS

In 1980 Rolf appeared in his first-ever pantomime, *Cinderella*, at the Lewisham Theatre, with Lorraine Chase as Cinders and Rolf playing the part of Buttons. Before his retirement from panto in 1996, Rolf appeared in fifteen further pantomime productions, including *Jack and the Beanstalk* and *Mother Goose*, at theatres all across Britain. Here, some of his colleagues from those shows remember their experiences with Rolf, starting with the man who coerced Rolf into panto in the first place, Paul Elliott. He's behind you!

PAUL ELLIOTT

Paul Elliott is the 'E' part of E&B Productions, Britain's most successful pantomime producers. Paul was instrumental in persuading Rolf that he would be the ideal star for the role of Buttons in 1980.

Although this may seem unbelievable now, it actually took quite a while to convince Rolf that panto would be right up his street. I think, being an Australian, he didn't entirely understand the medium. I had to sit down and talk with him on several occasions to help him accept that he would be master at the art because of his ability to connect with people. He has a wonderful one-to-one sincerity, and I thought he would be perfect at guiding an audience all the way through a show. Which, of course, he was, once I had managed to persuade him.

I got the measure of Rolf fairly early on. His career at that time was good, but he didn't have as high a profile as he had in either the Sixties or today. He was starring in *Cinderella* with Lorraine Chase, who was very hot property indeed at the time. Both Rolf's and Lorraine's agents were juggling for top billing. I was having a fairly heated discussion with Phyllis Rounce, Rolf's agent, when Rolf walked into the office and asked, 'What's the problem?'

I replied, 'It's the billing!'

'Easy peasy,' said Rolf, picking up a piece of paper. And he drew the billing on the paper. He said, 'I'll go there, down a bit, and she can go there, up a bit. That'll do, won't it? I'm happy with that, so get on with it!' Phyllis Rounce's face dropped! I think we were both astounded by this very judicious and wise man.

That was a great start, and Rolf went on to form an excellent partnership with the late Bill Owen from *Last of the Summer Wine*. They worked together for several years, developing a wonderful rapport, and having some tremendous seasons. In the early Nineties, when Rolf's television career was on the up again, I teamed him up with Lesley Joseph for *Cinderella* in Bath for what turned out to be a record season. We had 98 per cent capacity for the entire run, a record that is unlikely ever to be beaten.

After that pantomime, I said to him, 'Look, I don't know how to tell you this, but I think we're all getting a bit old. I know you think you're a young stud, but you're going to have to start playing the baron.' I called him a young stud because he always enjoyed chatting to the chorus girls. I asked him once, 'What would you do if one of the girls said, "Come on, Mr Harris, I really fancy you"?'

He laughed and said, 'I'd run a billion miles!'

Rolf agreed that maybe it was time for him to become the baron, but he said to me, 'I've been on the same money for seven years, any chance of a bit of a raise?'

I said, 'Put like that, Rolf, I'll tell you what I'll do: I'll send a blank contract to your agent, and you put in whatever figure you think is

BEN ... WONDERFUL TO TALK TO YOU AGAIN!

cheers

Rolf

right. I know you're a fair man, and I hope I am as well.' The contract came back with exactly the figure I'd thought it would be.

There are many reasons why Rolf was so successful in panto. For a start he is completely genuine and very sincere. There's a great affection between both Rolf and the audience and Rolf and his colleagues. He is always so fresh, and he gives the impression with each line that it is the first time he has ever delivered it. Everyone in an audience loves him, from the youngest child to the oldest grandparent.

Teaming up Rolf with Gary Wilmot was inspirational, although I say so myself! They were sensational together, but sadly, on their second season, Rolf was unwell and decided it was time to retire from pantomime. I think the pace caught up with him. Regrettably, I think we've lost him to the panto for ever, which is an incredibly sad loss. The theatres still ask for him each year, but I can understand his decision. When I'm seventy I won't want to be putting on pantomimes, let alone starring in them!

However, Rolf's legacy lives on. When he was in Plymouth doing *Jack and the Beanstalk* with Bonnie Langford, he painted a mural on the wall of his dressing room. Now, whoever has that dressing room has an original Rolf Harris all to themselves. Mind you, there is one artist, who shall remain nameless, who wouldn't play Plymouth. 'Why not?' I asked.

'I can't bear staring at Rolf Harris for six weeks!' he replied.

LORRAINE CHASE

When Rolf starred with Lorraine in his first pantomime it took him a little while to get used to the fact that pantomime is a team game, not a solo performance, where sticking to the script is essential for the smooth running of a show. For Lorraine, it was the only time she ever acted with Rolf, but it wasn't the only time she worked with him.

When Rolf and I performed together in panto, I played Cinderella to his Buttons. He was very sweet, but a little worried and nervous at the start because it was the first time he had ever performed in pantomime. I'd done Cinderella a couple of times before, but it was lovely working with Rolf. He had his own musical director, Barry Booth, who is a very jolly man who had worked with Rolf for many years and so was able to follow Rolf when necessary.

I remember one of the first nights very clearly. We used to do 'Six White Boomers' towards the end, with Rolf at the front while the rest of us did a quick costume change behind the curtain. On this particular evening someone in the audience shouted out 'Two Little Boys'. As his musical director knew all his songs, Rolf was able to launch into a piano-accompanied version without hesitation, as he was doubtless used to doing at his solo concerts. So instead of 'Six White Boomers' we heard him going into 'Two Little Boys'. Everyone assumed he would sing 'Boomers' afterwards, which would give us longer than

usual to change. But he didn't, and in the event, because 'Two Little Boys' is shorter, we actually had about thirty seconds less than normal. In panto, every second counts when it comes to costume changes. Rolf was obviously unaware of this and, as he finished the song, the curtains opened. Of course, half the singers and dancers were still trying to put their clothes on and sort themselves out. Rolf's face was a picture, and the poor love, he felt awful. He realized the confusion he'd thrown everyone into, so he got on the tannoy before the next show and apologized to the whole cast. He never made that mistake again!

The following year, I worked with Rolf again when we acted as announcers for the royal wedding of the Prince and Princess of Wales. Each presenter was on a different section of the route for the royal procession. He was at Australia House and I was on the next part, at Fleet Street. The night before the wedding all the presenters, including Terry Wogan and Richard Burton, stayed in the same hotel, as we had to get up very early the next morning. There was a small group of us, and it was lovely having a chance to see Rolf again. On the day of the wedding the procession got to Australia House first. We'd been told by the producers to be fairly straight-laced in our commentary as we were broadcasting worldwide. After the carriage had passed Australia House, Rolf was due to hand over to me. 'Lorraine, Lorraine, have you caught sight of them yet?' he asked.

I said, 'Rolf, I'm hanging out of the window of the Cross Keys in Fleet Street by my toenails and I still can't see them.' The next moment they came round the corner. 'Oh, yes, they're just coming round now,' I said. And then I got myself into such trouble. 'Look at them!' I said. 'Even the sun is shining for them, and it's shining on those lovely guards' helmets.' I realized immediately what I'd said, and waited for Rolf to help me out. For once he was caught on the hop; he was completely speechless. Rolf Harris silent, who would believe it? I think I stumbled on with something like, 'Oh, it's just so good to be British!'

Sadly, that was the last time we worked together. But if I could persuade him to come out of retirement, you never know, one day we might get to play the Uglies together!

GARY WILMOT

Gary Wilmot is probably the youngest veteran – or oldest youngster – of the entertainment profession in the UK today, and he starred with Rolf in his very last Cinderella. *Gary played Buttons, the part Rolf had started out with in 1980, to Rolf's Baron Hardup.*

Rolf Harris is a legend; there's no doubt about it. Everyone has fond memories of Rolf. Certainly when I was a child I used to love watching him on television, so having an opportunity to work with him was a real plus for me. We had a great time doing *Cinderella* together at the Birmingham Hippodrome. To have the chance to spend some time with Rolf during rehearsals was a real joy. I hadn't realized how big his heart is; Rolf is a real giver. It's amazing that somebody has lasted so long in this ruthless business when they give as much of themselves as Rolf does. Whenever we went on publicity tours to promote the show in Birmingham, Rolf was always on his mettle. We visited places like hospices and children's hospitals, and he would always be there with a song, anecdote, or a funny little game to play with the children.

My fondest memory of Rolf is quite bizarre. On the last night of rehearsals our director took us out for a meal. We went to an Indian restaurant and had a very enjoyable evening. Rolf had sung a few songs, as he always does, we had finished our meal, and the place was quite empty. Just as we were about to leave, in walked a gang of extremely drunken, raucous Birmingham lads. Our director suggested we make a hasty exit, but Rolf just took his time. We all got out without being recognized, except for Rolf. We ended up outside, waiting in the cold, while Rolf spent at least fifteen minutes in the restaurant with these lads. From outside we could hear loud cheering and singing. Our director dashed in and out, giving us reports of what was going on inside! Rolf was signing autographs, and even drew a Rolfaroo on one of these guy's behinds. He dropped his trousers in the restaurant and was bent over a chair while Rolf drew on his backside. I wouldn't be surprised if he had it tattooed the next day! That is typical of Rolf; he gets on with absolutely everyone.

In the theatre his dressing room was described as Geppetto's workshop. Rolf is a bit of an inventor, and he was always beavering away at something or other. At one point he was working on a coat hanger, and none of us had the heart to tell him they had already been invented.

Rolf has always been able to laugh at himself. When we were doing *Cinderella* he was invited to London to record a version of 'Bohemian Rhapsody', apparently with Queen's full approval. We all thought he was joking, but a couple of weeks later he came in with a rough mix of the track and played it for us. There must have been fifteen people in his dressing room, all of whom just sat there open-mouthed. We looked at one another in amazement when it started playing. The sound of 'Bohemian Rhapsody' with a wobble-board and Rolf's special breathing techniques providing the rhythms for the song was quite bizarre. At the end of it Rolf asked, 'What do you think?' We all burst out laughing, and he loved it; he could see the humour in it.

Rolf was wonderful to work with. He commands respect. In spite of his clothing, Rolf is an extremely sophisticated performer! He thinks very long and hard about what he does, but he's also instinctive. That may seem a contradiction in terms, but his instincts provide Rolf with the slick ease he utilizes to carry out his job as a performer and entertainer. Rolf and I had a special relationship in *Cinderella*. I could do anything on stage with Rolf, and he would go with me. I enjoyed being on stage with Rolf; it was a genuine pleasure. When all is said and done, Rolf Harris is simply a really nice bloke who wants world peace. And I think if he sticks around long enough, he'll get it.

BONNIE LANGFORD

Bonnie Langford played the principal boy in E&B's production of Jack and the Beanstalk *at the Plymouth Theatre in 1992. The all-star cast included Dame Hilda Brackett as Jack's mum, Carmen Silvera as the fairy godmother and a certain Rolf Harris in the role of Simple Simon.*

Long before we played in *Jack and the Beanstalk* together I'd performed with Rolf at various charity events. About fifteen years ago I was playing Peter Pan at the Aldwych Theatre, and was invited to perform a selection from the show for the Children's Royal Variety Performance at the Dominion. Rolf was asked to introduce me, and he did a wonderful thing. A cloth came down at the front of the stage, behind which I had to get into position. While introducing me he painted Wendy, Michael and John on the cloth, and as he finished he said, 'All clap your hands, because here comes the one person that's missing from this picture, and that's Peter Pan!' As the cloth went up it revealed more of the streets of London underneath, which he'd painted earlier. It was such a lovely, novel way of introducing the performance.

During the first few days of rehearsals for *Jack and the Beanstalk*, Rolf was over in Australia. When he came down to Plymouth his first priority was to get to know the children who were performing in the pantomime. It was lovely to see him with them, learning their names and chatting away. Rolf is a real sweetheart, and so funny; he used to come to rehearsals in his slippers. I'd have Patrick Fife on one side wearing high heels, and Rolf on the other wearing his sheepskin slippers. There was an amazing collection of shoes on that stage, and in addition to that Rolf would always be making his breathing noises;

sometimes they'd come out of nowhere and make me jump!

When we first started performances, there was a point towards the end of the show when Rolf would choose half a dozen children from the audience to join him. Once on stage he would talk to them about cartoons, and get them each to do a drawing while he chatted away to them. It was fascinating, but it could go on for ever. We'd all go off and have a cup of tea! By the time we came back to do the finale it felt like the next performance. It wasn't long before the director cut it down to only two children.

One evening a crowd from Rolf's fan club turned up at the show. I think a lot of them were from the naval college in Plymouth, and they all dressed up as Rolf. It was hilarious to see all these people wearing loud shirts and joke false beards. It was the most hysterical performance of the pantomime. When Rolf sang 'Stairway to Heaven' it was like one of his concerts. They all had wobble-boards, so they played and sang along.

Rolf is a very creative person; he's always doing something. I remember going to Plymouth on the train for a press call with Rolf. He had some stones and little sticks with him, and he spent the whole journey grinding and polishing these stones. The intensity of Rolf's interest in what he was doing was quite amazing. Rolf has an incredible passion for objects that we would consider to be normal, everyday things; and through his interest, we become interested. That is an important key to his charm and, I think, the reason Rolf is so successful when he presents TV programmes. I was watching him once on *Animal Hospital* when he was surrounded by dogs. He had a fit of the giggles, and it was so charming and natural. I don't think Rolf could ever do something he didn't believe in. He has to have a passion for what he's involved with. While we were doing *Jack and the Beanstalk*, ITV decided to cut his children's television show *Rolf's Cartoon Club*. He was very upset and spoke to me about it. But his disappointment wasn't so much for himself; it was because he believed in the show. He thought that his show gave children something that was really important: the chance to be calm, quiet and creative. Just like Rolf, in fact!

CARMEN SILVERA

Carmen Silvera, one of the other members of the cast from Jack *and the* Beanstalk *at the Theatre Royal in Plymouth, recalls clearly Rolf's off-stage pastime.*

Jack and the Beanstalk was one of the best panto productions I've ever seen or been involved with. It was a brand-new Paul Elliott production and the sets were magnificent, the costumes were marvellous and Rolf just added to everything. He was an absolute joy to work with; he was always so friendly and cheerful, and really inventive. The producers incorporated Rolf's songs into the production so, for example, when he sang 'Stairway To Heaven' we went up into cloud-land to the giant's castle. The set had great rainbows stretching right across the stage, diminishing into the distance; it looked as if they went on for ever, into eternity.

During the course of the run Rolf painted the most wonderful mural of the pantomime along the whole stretch of the star dressing-room wall. The wall was originally breeze block, but he had it plastered over before he started the painting and was a little impatient waiting for it to dry. Rolf is renowned for his three-minute landscapes, but this picture was different: it was incredibly detailed work. He depicted all the characters in the show, with me flying and Bonnie climbing up the beanstalk; there was Dame Trot's cottage, the giant's castle in the distance and all the countryside scenes, the rainbow and the clouds. It was wonderful. He worked in the tiniest detail and picked out the little things from the panto, those one wouldn't even have thought about. He painted in a lovely little river, with one of the dancers, who had a beautiful face, sitting next to it contemplating the water.

Rolf took a real pride in the painting. Sometimes he would go in early in the morning to work on it, and occasionally, during the show, he'd only just make it on stage in time, as he would sometimes paint when he was off-stage. The show ran for about six or seven weeks, and Rolf didn't quite manage to finish it all, so he went back afterwards, when the production had finished its run, to complete it. It's still there; it's the pride of the theatre, and I believe they used it as their Christmas card once.

JUNE WHITFIELD

June Whitfield starred as the fairy godmother and Rolf as the baron at the Wimbledon Theatre in Cinderella *in 1994.*

I gather Rolf is no longer doing pantomime. He has come to the conclusion that twelve shows a week is not a good idea. Such a wise man. I hung up my wings after Wimbledon, but I'm delighted they had their last airing with Rolf.

We were never actually on stage at the same time during *Cinderella*. Apart from in the finale! We used to meet at the bottom of the steps, waiting to go up together for the finish, usually muttering, 'Why are we doing this?' But on hearing the reception as we took our bows the question was answered.

I used to wait in the wings, ready to go on after Rolf's Jake the Peg. Although I watched very closely I could never fathom out which was the extra leg. I *knew* which it was because he showed me once. But when he was performing I could never really tell. It was brilliant. There's no doubt you need energy for panto and, my goodness, Rolf's got plenty of that.

He did a spectacular for television once, and I wandered on at the end, endeavouring to play the wobble-board. He gave me a quick lesson before the show and said it was all in the wrist. I think I probably managed to get it right once in every five beats.

I loved performing with Rolf. I thought he was an absolutely delightful man to work with. He's so sweet; he always had a smile and a joke about the place. Rolf's also an ace photographer; he's very keen.

He was never without his camera and snapped everybody. He must use a colour filter, because his photos have a mysterious, slightly pinky, mauvey look about them, which you wouldn't get with a Box Brownie! He gave me lots of photographs that he took of me on stage; me and the little fairies. I treasure those.

10

ADVISERS AND EQUERRIES

In terms of longevity and success, Rolf's career has been outstanding. Whilst this is undoubtedly down to a combination of his personality and considerable talents, behind every great star is a team that advises, steers and guides their career. Through the years Rolf has been managed by some of the finest individuals and companies in the business. During the Seventies he was looked after by International Artists and the formidable Phyllis Rounce. When Rolf's brother, Bruce, took overall control of Rolf's worldwide professional activities in the early Eighties, Rolf moved to London Management, where he was teamed up with the much-respected Billy Marsh. Billy then formed his own company, Billy Marsh Associates, who have been looking after Rolf's UK affairs ever since.

SYD GILLINGHAM

Syd Gillingham is an ex-Fleet Street journalist who worked on the Daily Telegraph *before moving to EMI Records as press officer in 1958. It was through EMI that Syd first worked with Rolf, on the promotion for 'Tie Me Kangaroo, Sport'. And he continued working as Rolf's press agent until 1993.*

In all my years of working in show business, Rolf Harris is one of the nicest people I have come across, if not *the* nicest! There are no airs and graces about Rolf, he never acts like a star and he is always sincere and genuine. But he is also one of the worst organized people I have ever met. When we worked together, which was for thirty-one years in total, we regularly used to have frantic searches for publicity pictures that I knew he had; it could take hours to find them. He would ring me up sometimes in, say, June or July, and would tell me he'd just found a letter someone had written to him last October, and ask what he should do about it. There was a notable time once when I took him to the airport. We arrived to find he'd forgotten his accordion and we had to go back for it. Another time we got there two hours early because he'd mistaken the time of the flight. That man really needs a twenty-four-hour personal assistant to organize him.

Rolf also needs a chauffeur with the patience of a saint to drive him. He's the world's worst back-seat driver. I actually threatened him once; I stopped the car and joked, 'Just get out and walk!' He was all right for the rest of the journey. Rolf's a very sensitive man; he dislikes any sort of confrontation. He will always walk away from a row, as I do, and that's doubtless one of the reasons we got on so well together.

I recall a time we went to the Birmingham National Exhibition Centre, where Rolf was due to paint a mural. I was wearing a new pair of Hush Puppies. They had erected scaffolding for Rolf to paint from, and we climbed up together and one of us – I always maintain it was him – stood on the end of a plank. It was straight out of the Laurel and Hardy school of slapstick. The paint went flying up in the air and landed all over my new suede shoes. To add insult to injury, the paint was pink!

Another time I remember coming back from Norwich on a train. Rolf doesn't normally drink, but on this occasion we went into the restaurant car. There was a table for four, and the window seats were taken by a mother and daughter. We sat on the outside and Rolf had a glass of red wine. For him, that was more than enough. He started to sing music-hall songs at the top of his voice, making everyone else in the carriage join in. It lasted the entire journey, and I'm sure, to this day, that the lady and her daughter still talk about it.

Rolf's mind is filled with old music-hall songs, not to mention jokes, most of which are quite blue. One of my favourites involved an old lady and an old man chatting at their retirement home. 'Guess how old I am,' said the man. The lady declined to guess, but the man persisted, saying he would help her guess in any way she wished. 'All right,' she said. 'Drop your trousers.' The old man was a bit surprised, but slowly rose to his feet and dropped his trousers. 'And your underpants,' she added. Reluctantly, he slowly dropped his underpants. She looked him up and down, walked around the back and then grabbed him where he least expected it! She looked him in the eye and said, 'I'd guess you were going to be ninety-one next Wednesday.' The old man couldn't believe it; she was absolutely right. 'Blimey!' he said. 'How did you know that?' And the old lady replied, 'You told me yesterday!'

Rolf is very giving of his time with people. He used to travel to Australia two or three times a year, and I normally went to the airport with him. On one occasion he had checked in his luggage and we were just wandering around. A young lad came up and started talking to us, and Rolf told him how to create simple animation with a pad of paper. He explained that you draw a figure slightly differently on each sheet, and when you flip through the pad it looks like an animated cartoon – the figure would appear to move. He explained all this to the boy, and then we took the lift to the floor below. As we alighted, Rolf realized there was something he had left out of his explanation, so he went back up in the lift and searched for the lad until he found him.

PHIL DALE

Phil Dale is a successful theatrical agent, who manages a diverse range of artists, including DJ Simon Bates. In the early Seventies Rolf was looked after by London Management, where Phil cut his teeth in the entertainment industry.

When Rolf joined London Management I was the new boy in the company and was quite nervous about meeting him. My apprehension was unfounded, as he is such a warm, charming man. We shared a cup of tea and Rolf was very natural. We didn't work together very often, although I put on one of his shows in Great Yarmouth, which was great fun.

After Rolf had left London Management, I remember going home from the office one evening on London Underground. It was about twenty past six and the tube was absolutely packed with commuters. I was up against the door between carriages, and I saw Rolf in the next compartment. We were both standing up, crammed against the window, and he spotted me. I made a gesture to wave, and he waved back, and that was that. With hindsight, I should have got off the train at

the next stop to go and say hello, but the train was full and Rolf is such a big star that I didn't think he'd want to be bothered by me. The next thing I knew, we pulled into Victoria, the carriage emptied and on jumped Rolf! He had left his carriage to join mine. He asked me how I was and what I was up to. I've never forgotten that.

Many years later, one of my clients, Simon Bates, rang me up and said, 'I've got this unbelievable recording of Rolf Harris.'

I said, 'Oh, he's a great man; I used to work with him. What is it?' He told me about 'Stairway to Heaven', and brought it in for me to hear. I said, 'Well, you're actually bringing it back to the office where Rolf originated; he used to be with us.' Simon played the tape and I howled with laughter. It was wonderful. I thought it was absolutely brilliant. Simon said he was going to plug it until it was released, which, of course, he did. I saw Rolf soon after and asked him how the recording had come about. He told me that when he was doing a TV show in Australia, they had asked him to perform the song, but he didn't know it. The record company offered to send him a copy of the Led Zeppelin classic, but he declined, saying that he only wanted the sheet music and lyrics so the original wouldn't influence his rendition. He actually recorded his version of the song without hearing Led Zeppelin's original. Wonderful stuff!

JAN KENNEDY

Jan Kennedy is managing director of Billy Marsh Associates, Rolf's agents and personal managers since the 1980s. Jan was instrumental in procuring the job for Rolf as Animal Hospital *presenter, an opportunity he nearly squandered at his first meeting!*

I've known Rolf all my life, but then, hasn't everyone? And I've worked closely with him for about fifteen years. When he first joined Billy Marsh Associates I was assigned, alongside Billy Marsh, to help with Rolf's career. My first impression of Rolf was of a man who is very warm and approachable. His objective wasn't to be a major star; that has never come into Rolf's thinking. His irrepressible enthusiasm was for his work; to do what he loves, and to do it well. His desire is still the same today: to entertain people of all ages and to make them happy.

Rolf's greatest failing is that he can never say no; he would do a charity function every day if he could. However, I am very respectful of Rolf's age; he may be seventy years young, but he can't do what a twenty-three-year-old can do. That doesn't stop him from trying sometimes, though! Over the years I have had to become more in-sistent that he stops to 'smell the roses' on occasions, to spend time with his family and even to take a holiday now and then.

In 1994 I received a phone call from Lorraine Heggessey at the BBC, who approached us with the idea of Rolf presenting their new show, *Animal Hospital*. Apparently, at that time, it was only Lorraine who really wanted Rolf; her colleagues weren't convinced that he was the right person for the job. I organized a lunch for Rolf to meet the production team.

Unfortunately, he had recently come back from a trip to Australia where he'd suffered from horrible vertigo as a result of an inner-ear infection. Consequently, his tour had to be cancelled and he had been treated with massive doses of steroids to clear up the virus. When he returned to the UK he was suffering from depression after coming off the necessary medication. He felt particularly low, and sat there throughout the whole lunch looking quite miserable and not saying a word. When we left the restaurant I said to him, 'If you get this job you'll be the luckiest man on earth.'

He replied, 'Why? What did I do wrong?'

I told him, 'It's not what you did, it's what you *didn't* do. You didn't say a word during that lunch.' When I got back to the office I rang the BBC, apologized and explained that Rolf had been unwell. Luckily they agreed to another meeting, and that time Rolf was feeling much better. He was on top form, absolutely wonderful, his totally natural self, and the rest, as they say, is history.

Animal Hospital has been fantastic for Rolf's career. It has added a brilliant new dimension to his vast public appeal by showing his genuine care and love for animals. With the warmth of Rolf's personality, the success of *Animal Hospital* has exceeded everyone's expectations. I knew it would do well because the formula was wonderful, but I don't think anyone dreamed it would have the longevity and success that it has.

It's always amazing to see the extent of the affection and love that people have for Rolf. I went to the closing ceremony of the Rugby World Cup Final with him at the new Millennium Stadium in Wales. As Australia were in the final, Rolf sang on the pitch for his country before the game. The welcome and response he received were phenomenal. Afterwards, we walked from the stadium together to the official reception for the teams, and on the way we were mobbed by people of all nationalities, shaking Rolf's hand, hugging and slapping him on the back. As we were walking through the streets I said, 'I feel truly emotional.'

He said, 'It's lovely, isn't it, kid?' and he had tears in his eyes. Rolf really is unique.

It was fabulous when we did *This is Your Life* for Rolf. I was adamant that I wanted the moment when Michael Aspel appears with his red book to be a special pick-up. As well as all his other talents, Rolf is a brilliant musician, so I came up with the idea of surprising him in Edinburgh, where Rolf was to head a parade of 3,000 marching bag-pipe players. He was to lead them down Princes Street in aid of the Marie Curie Cancer Care fund. Rolf had learned to play the bagpipes especially for the occasion and was fitted out with the most fantastic kilt. After the rehearsal, he pulled me to one side and said, 'I've got to have a word with you. I can't play these bloody bag-pipes properly. I can get a sound, but I can't master it.'

'Just play it from the heart,' I said, 'and do the best you can.' So Rolf paraded up Princes Street blowing his bagpipes – goodness knows what was coming out of them – leading 3,000 pipers. At the end, to Rolf's complete surprise, Michael Aspel brought out the red book. It was a wonderful moment; very emotional.

I have tremendous admiration, pride and love for Rolf. We all do. The girls in our office adore him because he never forgets them; he's generous to everybody. There will never be another Rolf Harris; he's a one-off.

LISA RATCLIFF

Lisa Ratcliff is personal assistant to Jan Kennedy at Billy Marsh Associates, and accompanies Rolf on many of his assignments.

When I was young I had an uncle who lived in Australia, and my grandparents visited him each year. When they returned they would usually bring us back a traditional Australian present, like a cork hat or a koala bear. One year I remember my brother and I being given a Stylophone each, with a Rolf Harris record and instruction book to accompany them. We would play them while my grandfather sang 'Jake the Peg'. That was my first introduction to Rolf, and over the next few years I became a great fan of his.

It feels quite strange now that I work with Rolf, dealing with his diary and all his engagements, and speaking to him regularly on the phone. The first time I met him I was quite nervous; I think I was worried about what to say. But Rolf was so friendly and warm that he put me at ease immediately.

Rolf is so busy; he does so many things in such a diverse number of professional areas. He is constantly in demand and supports many charities. Rolf is the president of Phab; he's involved in Chatha, a charity that takes animals into hospitals for children; he does work for the Epilepsy Foundation and numerous other charitable organizations. He simply loves to be occupied.

Rolf is incredibly lucky to have the support of his wife, Alwen. She is an enchanting character, with her beautiful braided hair and the jewellery she makes. I went to a function with her and Rolf in Cardiff, where Rolf was collecting a Welsh Hall of Fame award from the Royal Television Society. He made a lovely speech; it brought tears to everyone's eyes, including his, and in it he thanked Alwen for her support. Looking at the pair of them, I realized how well suited they are; they're the perfect match.

PAT LAKE-SMITH

Pat Lake-Smith has worked as Rolf's press agent since 1993, when she first promoted and publicized his new-found success on the university concert circuit. With the arrival of Animal Hospital *the following year, keeping Rolf in the public eye has never been much of a problem for her!*

Rolf is exceedingly easy to market. He is at the forefront of almost everything, and on prime-time television. Whenever a story connected with animals, Australia, beards, art or music hits the headlines, a quote from Rolf is required. He is officially one of the most prominent entertainers and artists on the planet! In 1998, *Time* magazine organized a worldwide poll and, in the section for entertainers, Rolf Harris ranked amongst the top ten. Frank Sinatra didn't even get a look in, although it was suspected that college students voting on the *Time* Internet website were responsible for the massive support for Rolf! In 1992, there was a survey in Britain which asked a thousand people to name a well-known artist. 38 per cent chose Rolf Harris. Constable got 23 per cent of the vote while Rembrandt and Turner didn't even make the frame! Although Rolf will point out that they didn't have their own TV series at the time.

When I started working with Rolf it was at a time when his image was changing, and the main thrust of my job was to make the public aware of that fact. He had just started to perform at university gigs and had had a huge hit with 'Stairway to Heaven', and it was important that we publicize the reaction the students were giving him. We had some classic situations where youngsters were fainting at his gigs. They weren't fainting because they were in awe of Rolf; they were fainting because they were packed to the rafters and it was intensely hot, but, of course, being able to say that students were passing out at Rolf Harris gigs was a tremendous help in changing the public's perception of Rolf.

One of his great strengths is that he hasn't hardened himself against the world. He's not afraid to show his innocence and awe of life. And he genuinely likes people. He is never patronizing; no matter who he's talking to, he treats everyone the same. When he is interviewed he'll answer every question as if for the first time, with great consideration, care and detail, whether it's for a student magazine or an international publication. One of the questions Rolf is most frequently asked is whether he has ever considered shaving off his beard. His answer is that he did once, before he and Alwen were married. She was horrified and said he looked like an American car with all the chrome removed; she told him to grow it back again quick!

His unpretentious attitude is extended to his clothes. When photographer Chris Christodoulou asked Rolf if perhaps he should take some more formal photographs and asked if he had a suit, Rolf replied, 'I've heard the bloomin' things exist, but I don't own one!'

Rolf's seemingly boundless energy is, in fact, down to his amazing ability to go into total repose whenever he has the opportunity. This conserves his energy for the moment it is required. Recently, when he was relaxing in his dressing room on *This Morning*, he was startled out of his reverie when fellow guest Tony Bennett sauntered in and turned the tables on him. He asked if he could sketch Rolf. Rolf was taken aback: he is usually the one who does the sketching.

11

ROYAL BOUNTY

Rolf is president of the charity Phab, founded over forty years ago to help break down some of the barriers faced by disabled people and to give them the same opportunities as their able-bodied friends. Rolf is also patron of a number of charities, and he regularly attends events throughout the year for a whole range of causes. Whatever the occasion, he is always very hands-on, giving himself fully and getting involved in the thick of things.

SIR CLIFF RICHARD

Sir Cliff Richard was the original president of Phab when the charity started, and he still supports the organization today. Alongside Rolf, Cliff is probably the only performer in the UK who has sustained a successful career spanning each decade since the Fifties.

Rolf is one of those people who sit firmly in the middle of every area of entertainment. One moment he will be seen presenting an animal show, the next minute he's doing quick-fire drawings for children's TV, and then he's at the top of the charts. He is also president of the charity Phab, which is an incredibly valuable thing to do. For Rolf to be prepared to give up his time and put his name to an organization that draws the able-bodied and disabled together is fantastic. I have great respect for him for taking on that job.

Rolf's career has been quite amazing, and he's now part of the showbiz furniture. Everyone remembers Rolf's biggest hits; they're unforgettable. 'Tie Me Kangaroo Down, Sport' was fun, 'Sun Arise' was a really good pop record, but 'Two Little Boys' was a truly great pop record. There's no doubt about the emotional feeling for that song, and it was released at just the right time. It was a Christmas number one at the end of the Sixties, and was still number one at the turn of the decade. Although it's not a Christmas song, it has all the right sentiment and emotion. I always admire people who can choose the moment. We all try to do it, but we don't always get it right. In Rolf's case, 'Two Little Boys' was perfectly timed, and he had a deservedly huge number one record.

What is so astonishing about the success of his songs is that Rolf is never perceived as a pop star, yet he bursts in every now and then with a huge hit. He fits into all sorts of categories. A song like 'Jake the Peg', which I saw him perform on *The Royal Variety Show*, is typical of what you might expect from a top comedian, but again, Rolf isn't perceived as a comedian, despite being able to deliver a very funny performance of a very funny song. It's quite amazing that he is able to turn his hand to so many areas of entertainment. That's what I like about Rolf; he's always there, and he has my lasting admiration for that.

JOHN CORLESS

John Corless is the honorary chairman of Phab. As president of Phab, Rolf has done much more than simply lend his name to the cause.

In the Phab brochure there is a quote from Rolf that sums up perfectly the objective behind Phab. 'Our aim is to give disabled people the same social opportunities that are enjoyed by able-bodied people, to bring them all together on equal terms.' Overall, that aim involves promoting and encouraging people with and without physical dis-abilities to achieve complete integration in the community.

As a charity, Phab was created in 1957, when a disabled young man named Terry Rolf, who regularly found himself unable to join in activities with his able-bodied friends, made the comment, 'I want opportunity, not pity.' This led to an organization being set up to create social clubs where disabled and able-bodied people could get together for all manner of activities. Since then, the charity has been instrumental in helping to change attitudes over the last forty years, so that these days the wider community is far more aware of the needs of disabled people. There are now over 350 clubs in the United Kingdom, and members' ages range from two to 106!

Rolf first came to a Phab function about twenty years ago, when I invited him to be guest of honour at a fund-raising lunch given by the Publicity Club of London. At that time Jimmy Saville was president, having succeeded Sir Cliff Richard. Jimmy decided to step down as president of Phab in order to concentrate on his Stoke Mandeville Appeal. It came as a bit of a shock, as I knew it would be difficult to replace him, but I thought I would approach Rolf because he had supported us in the past. To my immense delight, he accepted my invitation, but on the proviso that he would only do it for a year. Twelve years on he's still president!

Rolf is dedicated to Phab. For one of our brochures I wrote some copy for Rolf to approve. I wrote, 'Welcome to Phab, may I introduce myself as Phab's president.' When he returned the copy he had altered it to, 'Welcome to Phab. Let me say at the outset that I am most honoured to be president of Phab.' Rolf is a wonderful ambassador for this organization, and he believes in it wholeheartedly. When he attends a Phab event, the local press or television regularly interview him, and all his answers to their questions come from the heart. Rolf not only supports Phab; he understands its philosophy and believes in it.

Each year Rolf attends a variety of different Phab events, for example, the Heartbeat Hike, which is an annual gathering of Phab members and friends in Hyde Park. It is primarily a sponsored walk around the Serpentine by members to raise funds for their individual clubs. Rolf always attends, and is very instrumental in attracting a large number of people. Last year, in his capacity as president of Phab, Rolf came to the London Marathon when we had a team of over 200 runners. He attends presentation evenings, when he comes to receive cheques on behalf of the charity, and Disability Awareness Days, and he has also opened some of our centres.

It's always wonderful to watch Rolf at functions. He introduces himself to as many people as he can. Some of our members have speech problems, but Rolf will sit with families and take the time to listen to everyone. He has told me how aware he is of the changes in people's attitudes over the years. He remembers how, in his childhood, people were frightened by disability. Now he can see that, through organizations like ours, there have been very positive changes. Nowadays, disabled people are accepted as equals in the community. Rolf himself has contributed to that acceptance in a very big way.

BARBARA BATE

Barbara Bate is the organizer of the annual Young Pavement Artist of the Year competition, which raises funds for the Muscular Dystrophy Campaign. In 1999 the prize-giving was held at the Tate Gallery, with the prizes being awarded by a certain Rolf Harris Esq. Here, Barbara recounts just how involved Rolf becomes when he attends a function.

Rolf Harris to present the awards? You're mad; there's no chance! Mad I may be, but there's no harm in asking. The Young Pavement Artist of the Year competition is a national event, and only one young artist is chosen, with three runners-up.

Rolf answered my plea and said yes. The great day dawned and we eagerly awaited his arrival. Eventually, I spied him in the courtyard of the Tate Gallery. What a relief! He came as if from the TV screen, the customary twinkle in his eyes and a beaming smile. This lovable, homely man was immediately one of us. As soon as he appeared, the young artists gathered round, eager to speak to him and ask questions. When the proceedings started, he melted into a quiet corner.

The awards were a very natural affair. Rolf talked to each of the four winners, drawing them out, discussing their pictures and their hopes for the future. There were no nerves; everyone was completely relaxed. Rolf ensured that it would be *their* special day. He talked to us all about the art of drawing, and the fact that everyone has an innate ability to translate onto paper the joys around us. He then gave an impromptu song and dance, which brought the house down.

The most touching moment of the day came as Adam Myers, who has Duchenne muscular dystrophy, presented Rolf with a picture. Rolf didn't tower over Adam in his wheelchair, but knelt beside him, threw an arm around his shoulders and talked. Adam is shy and wary of people's reactions, as he is unable to move his hands. Talking to Rolf, we could see him quickly relaxing, no longer hesitant, but as if he were talking to an old friend.

Once the presentation was over, while the buffet lunch was being set out, Rolf spoke individually to the winners, their parents and friends. Oliver, the Young Pavement Artist of the Year, wants to be a cartoonist. With Rolf in reach, it was a golden opportunity not to be missed. 'To draw a face,' said Rolf, holding Oliver's mother by the chin, 'you need to realize that every face is lopsided. If you want to do a caricature, look for the lopsidedness and accentuate it. See, your mum smiles slightly more to this side than that. Try to capture that.' Oliver's mum didn't seem to mind having her face dissected; she was happy to let Rolf give her son a lesson, showing him how to create a caricature.

Rolf signed the back of all the framed prize drawings, and afterwards I tentatively asked if he would draw a cartoon on paper plates for the winners as an extra-special bonus to take home. There wasn't one moment of hesitation; the signing began. To my horror it continued for over an hour, as parents and all those present begged Rolf for a plate. He never even managed to eat his lunch! He was there to help make the day one to remember. Nothing was rehearsed; Rolf was his natural self and the young artists were the stars. He just made sure their day was filled with happy memories which would never be forgotten. His love and interest in both humans and animals are boundless.

12

SUBJECTS AND COURTIERS

Members of Rolf's fan club come from all generations and all walks of life. In addition to the vast numbers of student fans who regularly attend Rolf's gigs, adorned with beards, glasses and 'tasteful shirts', there are families, parents, children – not to mention cartographers and historians – who would love nothing more than to go walkabout with Rolf.

TONY CORDWELL

Tony Cordwell is Rolf's accountant. But far more interesting than that, Tony looks after the Rolf Harris Fan Club, PO Box 396, Northampton NN5 6ZW, which he founded in 1996. He is also the main brain behind Rolf's website, www.rolfharris.com, which receives over 2,000 hits a month.

I've worked with Rolf for some years now, and I recall, early on in our relationship, passing comment on a song he had recorded that I didn't like. To my surprise and delight he was very receptive to my remark. 'Great!' he said. 'That's what I want to hear. I don't like being surrounded by "yes men", I want to know about it if you don't like something.' I've worked that way ever since, though fortunately it's not that often that I feel the need to criticize.

Rolf has an amazing amount of knowledge about a wealth of different subjects. Since working with him, I've discovered it's not so much that he is well informed, it's that he seeks out information. If he doesn't know about a subject, he asks. When we were creating his website, he didn't really comprehend how it worked, and he asked so many questions that, in the end, I had to give him a crib sheet to help him understand it.

Rolf has had a website since 1996, but in May 1999 we completely revamped it. Rolf was very helpful with that. The original concept we based the site on was mine, with Rolf as the Wizard of Aus, guiding visitors around. At times, I don't think Rolf understood why I wanted certain things. For example, there are bits of simple animation on the website, with Rolfaroos hopping up and down, and these give the site an individual stamp. He was very helpful about producing these, without really understanding how we could use them. Of course, now

'We're not going to hurt one another . . . are we?'

he can see the point, and I think we're all very happy with the way the site looks and the enormous number of visitors it attracts. The record number of hits is 1,000 in one day, though that was when Rolf gave out the site address on *The Big Breakfast*.

There are plenty of original Rolf Harris cartoons on the website, but we only put the wholesome ones on display! Rolf does a great line in what I can only describe as 'adult' cartoons. On the wall of my office I have a Rolf original, which is a picture of a woman lying in a dentist's chair. The dentist is leaning over her with a drill in his hand and a panic-stricken look in his eye. Her hand is dangling off the edge of the chair and has a very firm grip on the dentist's nether regions. She is looking the dentist in the eye, and the caption reads, 'We're not going to hurt one another . . . are we?'

For me, the most important aspect of Rolf is not his art, his music, his TV shows, or his animals; it is his humanity. When people discover I work with Rolf, the first question is always, 'Oh, is he the same in the flesh as he comes across on the television?' It's great to be able to answer, 'Well, actually, he's even nicer than he seems to be.'

THE MORGAN FAMILY

Rolf has a special place in the hearts of all the Morgan family. Here they explain how supportive Rolf was at a time when they really needed it.

Our son Nick has Down's syndrome, not that that fact has ever come into the equation for Rolf. Nick is Nick, and he is who he is, a person in his own right, but having Down's syndrome means he sometimes puts things in such a simplistic way that they can appear quite profound. When I asked him what he would say if he were asked about Rolf he replied, 'Well, I think he is a real star; he cares about people.' He added, 'He's so interesting when I talk to him. It's like reading a book, but it's Rolf!' I asked Nick what his feelings were towards Rolf, and he said, 'Well, I love my family, and I love Rolf.' I asked, 'Do you love lots of other people then?' And he said, 'I like lots of other people.' So, for Nick, Rolf is on a par with his family.

Nick first met Rolf ten years ago. Rolf had fascinated him on the television, and he was appearing at St David's in Cardiff. Unfortunately, Nick was extremely sick at the time; he had to spend some time in isolation as a child. He wasn't allowed to go near anybody as every cold he picked up compromised his heart. Nick would have given his right arm to see Rolf, but he couldn't, so we phoned up St David's and left a message for Rolf. It was the first contact we made with him.

A few months later, out of the blue, a letter arrived for Nick from Rolf, saying that he was coming up to Merthyr Tydfil to open a wing of the museum where a painting of his grandfather's was exhibited. He wrote, 'I can see on the map that it's not far from you. Could you come down and meet me?' We took Nick to meet Rolf in the lord mayor's parlour, away from everybody. There was just the lady mayor and her grandchild, Rolf, Bindi and Alwen, and Nick and our daughter Lizzie, who also had Down's syndrome. I can remember Rolf scooping Nick up, and Nick's first words to him were, 'I like your hair,' as he stroked it. We had nearly an hour together, and when we came home, Lizzie said that Rolf was the best fun she'd ever met! She also thought Bindi was beautiful, with her long blond hair. So Nick liked Rolf's hair and Lizzie liked Bindi's!

That was our first meeting with Rolf, nearly ten years ago, and he has kept in touch ever since. We visited Rolf and Alwen at home once. Nick is terrified of dogs and Rolf brought his dog Summer out. He had to work so hard before Nick would put even a little finger on Summer. However, he didn't give up; Rolf must have brought every rule of psychology into play that day. Eventually he did it, and Nick left their home having stroked Summer!

Rolf adored Lizzie; she was stunningly beautiful, with long red hair and huge eyes. She was the healthiest of our four children, and she promoted awareness of people with Down's syndrome UK-wide. She was an amazing young person. About seven years ago Lizzie contracted a very rare form of cancer which was horribly aggressive. Although she had all the best treatment, she was twenty-seven when she died, and still absolutely beautiful.

When Lizzie was ill, Rolf came to visit her at our house. It wasn't planned; he just knew she was seriously ill and was being nursed at home as much as possible. He phoned one morning and said that he was on his way over with Hugh, his brother-in-law. He called in and sang to Lizzie and drew her some pictures. We had some food on the table, rolls and fillings, and I said, 'Rolf, what are you going to have to eat?' He said, 'Look, I'll put some of these things in a roll.' I replied, 'It's OK, I'll do it for you.' But he insisted, 'No, you go on, girl. I'll do it.' And he sat at the kitchen table making up rolls. As my eldest daughter pointed out, his talents have brought him fame and fortune, but he has never stopped being a man with soul. He might be incredibly famous, but he can still sit at a friend's table and make sandwiches.

Rolf was actually Lizzie's last visitor. After he had left our home, Lizzie was taken back into hospital for more tests. The day after the tests Lizzie started to lose her brave, brave battle.

Rolf was away when we held Lizzie's memorial service. She had taught all her nieces and nephews every nursery rhyme and song she knew, and the last two songs she taught them were 'Puff The Magic Dragon' and 'Two Little Boys'. Rolf recorded 'Two Little Boys' and sent a message to Lizzie on a tape, which we played at the service. In a way, because he was close to the family, Rolf shared our grief, which was incredibly helpful to us. He was desperately upset about the whole thing. Before Lizzie died, Rolf sent her and Nick a card from Australia. On it he wrote, 'Dear ones,' which tickled Lizzie pink. She absolutely treasured that; it's still with her belongings now.

After Lizzie died we received over 500 letters, and, although we saved every one, we never counted the cards. In one letter someone wrote that Lizzie was a gift to everyone. I think that's right; there are people who are a gift to everyone – people like Nick, people like Lizzie and people like Rolf.

CHRIS WOODALL

Chris Woodall is probably Rolf's longest-standing fan, though, as she likes to point out, that doesn't make her his 'oldest' fan! Chris's knowledge of Rolf, and her collection of Rolf memorabilia, which dates back to his early summer seasons in Great Yarmouth, is extensive.

In 1963, the fashion for young teenage girls was autograph hunting, and that was the pastime my friends and I pursued. Through it I became friends with a young singer named Mark Wynter, who did a summer season with Rolf at Great Yarmouth. The following year I went to Mark's twenty-first birthday party, and Rolf and Alwen were guests. We chatted, and during the course of the conversation Rolf said that he was returning to Yarmouth for the next summer season. When I told him I was holidaying there, he suggested I pop round and say hello, which, of course, I did. Our association dates from then. He's got us tickets for various TV shows over the years, and I used to go backstage to see him.

In the late Sixties I met my husband, Keith, and one evening, when we were watching television, Rolf was on and Keith wondered out loud how Rolf had got the idea for the wobble-board. I told him, but he didn't believe I'd found out from Rolf himself. I persuaded him to take me to Coventry, where Rolf was performing, so I could introduce him, but he was convinced he was being conned. He even got as far as the stage door still expecting to be thrown out, but, of course, we weren't, and Keith and Rolf hit it off straight away. When Keith was very ill in 1975 we saw quite a lot of Rolf; he was very supportive.

We used to go and watch Rolf at the Talk of the Town nightclub – at the time a top-class cabaret venue. The club was always packed out and the shows were fantastic. They had a slightly more adult content than his children's television shows, though he had to be a little careful because sometimes people did bring their children along.

For Rolf, the Talk of the Town show helped him secure his big break on evening television. There was an entertainer called Vicki

Carr, who was meant to be doing a BBC TV special. She suddenly had to go to hospital for an operation on her throat, and the BBC decided to film Rolf's show at the Talk of the Town instead. They brought the orchestra that was booked for Vicki Carr to the club, so it was a very extravagant show. Up until then, Rolf had only really been known as a children's host on television. But because it went so well, it led to *The Rolf Harris Show* with the Young Generation. Vicki was a guest on that once, and Rolf thanked her for unwittingly giving him his break.

As well as knowing about virtually all of Rolf's career, I'm a bit of a collector of Rolf Harris memorabilia. I still have tapes of some of his early radio shows from the Sixties. He used to do a ten-o'clock show in the morning, which was called *The Light Programme*. He would have different guests on each week, people like Cilla Black, Vera Lynn or Harry Secombe. Rolf sang all sorts of songs and would perform duets with his guests. In those days, Laurie Holloway was his accompanist.

I did start off as a fan, and obviously I still am. But the thing with Rolf is that he's so warm and giving, and I have met him so many times now, that what started as fanship has become a friendship.

ADELE BRODERICK

By contrast, Adele Broderick is one of Rolf's youngest fans.

I grew up watching programmes like *Rolf's Cartoon Club*, and was always fascinated by the way Rolf seemed to genuinely love drawing. He always had a way of captivating the viewer with his cheerful manner and soothing voice.

I became a fan of Rolf's from those days onwards. Seeing Rolf live on stage for the first time back in 1995 was an amazing experience. I shouldn't have been there – I was far too young to go to nightclubs – but the atmosphere was incredible and I got a real buzz from seeing

HEY KIDS !
DRAW WHAT **YOU**
THINK MIGHT BE

'**FUN** ᴵᴺ ᵀᴴᴱ **JUNGLE**'

maybe swingin' through
the trees with the
chimpanzees...
or, what a thriller, to
meet a gorilla!
an attack of the shakes
with some snakes maybe?
GET IT DOWN ON PAPER !
cheers...
Rolf Harris

the crowd cheering and jumping up and down to every song. I've been attending Rolf's gigs regularly ever since, and in every one of his performances he sings his heart out, as do the audience.

A few years ago I attended a talk Rolf was giving in London on the art of cartooning. I arrived about half an hour early, and was waiting quietly when I heard Rolf's voice in the corner of the room. It was a huge shock; somehow I'd expected him to make a grand entrance, with bodyguards in tow. Yet there he was, looking over some children's artwork before the talk began, chatting to anyone who approached him. That wasn't the only shock I had. During the talk, Rolf drew a quick sketch of me to demonstrate the art of drawing faces. And at the end of the evening he gave me the portrait he'd done.

My favourite meeting with Rolf was when he was signing copies of his latest book at a local shopping centre. Whilst waiting in the queue, my friend bet me ten pounds that I couldn't see Rolf without saying, 'I love you, Rolfie!' I was determined not to say it, until I came face to face with him and just couldn't resist. 'Er, thank you,' came Rolf's reply. I then got a bit too cocky for my own good and added, 'So how about a kiss then?' I thought I was being really clever until Rolf got up and gave me a big smacker in front of hundreds of people and said, 'That'll teach you!' I went a shade of purple and tried not to notice all the smiling faces as I skulked past them in a state of high embarrassment.

Ever since then I've become renowned for visiting Rolf at his signings, giving him a kiss and rushing off. I'm not sure if he minds or not, but if he did, I don't think he'd say so; he always has time for everyone. I'm proud to be a lifelong fan of someone like Rolf because, apart from being a very funny man, he treats everyone with respect and always gives everything he's got, whatever he's doing. Rolf, you're the best!

13

PEERS OF THE REALM

Over the years Rolf has touched the hearts of millions and has made many friends along the way. Those friends include some of the biggest show business names from the past forty years. He has also gained the respect and admiration of those who have enjoyed his unique talents while working with him on a variety of shows and recordings.

Here, some of Rolf's peers from the UK entertainment industry remember their shared times together and pay tribute to King Rolf, starting with one of Rolf's longest-standing friends and colleagues, Val Doonican.

VAL DOONICAN

Like Rolf himself, Val Doonican started out his professional career in the Fifties, presenting radio shows on the BBC. He soon progressed to become one of the most successful TV presenters of his generation, regularly host-ing shows through the Sixties, Seventies and Eighties.

Rolf Harris fits into the category of people in our business that I call one-offs. By that, I mean stars who are originals and are very different from their colleagues in the entertainment industry. Roy Castle was another example of a one-off. And the difference with characters like

Rolf and Roy is that they never follow the trend; they just do their own thing in their own unique way.

I've known Rolf over forty years, and it's quite remarkable, our careers have run pretty much in tandem all the way. We both started out presenting our morning radio programmes for the BBC, which is where we first met. In those days records weren't played on the show. Each presenter had their own little orchestra or band in the studio, and we talked and sang requests. I had a programme on Tuesday mornings and Rolf presented the equivalent programme on Thursday mornings. We regularly met up to confer about what we were doing. We both tended to enjoy singing novelty numbers, so we would liaise to make sure we didn't tread on each other's toes.

As a result, we became great friends. When we embarked on summer seasons we would often be in the same town at different theatres, so once again we'd meet up. Then, at the same time as I transferred to television, Rolf did too. We both used to host our own Saturday evening shows. I would do a run of thirteen shows, then someone like Cilla Black would do a series, then the Black and White Minstrels, and then *The Rolf Harris Show* would have a run. Once again we used to liaise, and Rolf would appear on my show and I would appear on his.

I remember him once appearing with his daughter, Bindi. Although I never used to do it on my shows, I enjoy drawing and painting. Rolf used to look at some of the things I did, but he's a bit of a critic! He'd say things like, 'You shouldn't do that, mate. I'll show you how to do it.' Anyway, Bindi is a beautiful artist. She came on the show with Rolf and, while I sang the David Gates song 'Daughter', she did a portrait of me, and Rolf did a cartoon.

I can also remember seeing Rolf attempt to play the Jew's harp on a show once, but he wasn't playing it properly. I enjoyed telling him so, especially after the criticism he used to give me about my painting! He wasn't holding it correctly, or getting the breathing effect right. I said to him, 'You're blowing it too hard; you're trying to play the didgeridoo on it. Just go easy and breathe the melody into it, and the tune will blow out lovely and loud.' He did as I said and has been doing it ever since.

When we first met, Rolf had never been to Ireland. I come from the south coast, from a place called Waterford. When we went out for dinner we would tell each other stories of our childhood and youth, and he became quite enamoured with the idea of visiting my hometown. So when Rolf finally went over to Ireland to perform, he very kindly went down to Waterford and called on my mum, Agnes. She was quite an old lady then and living in a nursing home.

One of the things about Rolf is that he is a real extrovert. I'm the opposite; so if Rolf were to be described as being over the top, then I'd be under the bottom! Everything he does is done at 150 miles an hour. As a matter of fact, when I was singing a duet with Rolf, I told him that singing with him was like farting against thunder, which is an old Irish expression my dad often used. In addition to being so outgoing, Rolf was very beardy in those days, with bushy hair and paint all over his clothes. My poor old mum was a terribly prim and proper lady, bless her, and Rolf apparently went into the nursing home roaring, 'How're you going, Aggie?' He put his arms around her and virtually lifted her out of the bed. She was about eighty-four at the time! When I next saw her I said, 'Did you like Rolf?'

She replied, 'Oh, he is such a lovely man; he was wonderful. But he should tidy himself up!'

Soon afterwards I started to do tours in Australia, and when I went to Perth I decided I must go and visit Rolf's mum and dad in Bassendean. I went out to their house for dinner and we sat in the sunshine and talked. They absolutely adored Rolf. They were real characters, just like the man himself! Rolf's father was called Cromwell, shortened to Crom. He told me that Marge, Rolf's mum, had said he mustn't tell me his full name was Cromwell, because of Oliver Cromwell's part in Irish history. Rolf and I had a good laugh about that later.

Rolf's parents were wonderful, such gorgeous people. They treated me so affectionately, and whenever I went to visit them, which I did each time I went to Australia, I felt as if I was calling on another part of my own family. After many years, I was due to visit them again when Rolf told me quietly, 'My mother doesn't know, but Crom has cancer.' In those days I used to smoke a pipe, and we were all chatting away, having tea beside the river, when I realized I'd left my tobacco at the hotel. Crom said, 'I've got to go down to the shops, would you like to come with me and buy some tobacco in town?' I jumped in the car with him and we headed down to the local shops. While we were driving, Crom said, 'By the way, I don't know if Rolf told you, but I've got cancer and it's not good. I don't know how long I've got, but Marge doesn't know about it, so please don't mention it.' We talked about the illness, and when we got back Crom went into the kitchen.

Marge and I sat outside, and she gently leaned over, confidentially patting my hand. She said, 'By the way, Val, Crom's got cancer, and he doesn't know I know. Honestly, Val, I don't know what I'm going to do; I really don't know how I'm going to live without him.' It just broke my heart, it really did, because they were such a wonderful couple who desperately loved and needed each other.

Some time later Crom died, which broke Rolf's and Bruce's hearts, as well as their mother's. After that I continued to visit Marge every year in her nursing home, where we would chat for ages about Crom. Sadly, after a while she passed away, too, and ever since then Rolf and I have a mutual understanding of our loss, because we were so close to each other's families.

CHRIS TARRANT

Chris Tarrant has had the pleasure of having Rolf as a guest on his show on a number of occasions. He also almost had the pleasure of being his next-door neighbour.

The last time the Capital Radio Breakfast Show team and myself flew down to Australia, we arrived in Perth late one night, understandably exhausted, having been bouncing around in the skies for over twenty-four hours. We walked into the nearest bar to the airport and were immediately greeted by a loud, heavy Oz voice saying, 'Hiya, Tarrant!' The engineers, my producer and myself all looked at each other and went, 'Oh no, it's Rolf Harris!' And we were right, it was. There he sat, larger than life, with a huge grin on his unmistakable face, looking out through his beard like a man peeping over a hedge. It was as if he were part of some bizarre welcoming ceremony that they arranged for all British visitors. It was, of course, pure coincidence but, bearing in mind that we'd been watching him on *Animal Hospital* in the airport lounge back in Britain just the day before, it was all very strange.

Another strange thing about Rolf – and there are many – is that everyone seems to know all his songs. Michael Parkinson organizes a special annual cricket match near his home in the village of Bray in Berkshire every summer. For no reason that I can think of, except that he lives just round the corner, Mike always gets Rolf to do the teatime entertainment. It's always a huge event and, if the weather's good, tens of thousands of people come to see all manner of celebrities play cricket. And there, in the sunshine, is Rolf, plus accordion and didgeridoo, going through the entire repertoire of 'Tie Me Kangaroo Down, Sport', 'Two Little Boys', 'Jake the Peg' and his cringe-making cover version of Led Zeppelin's immortal 'Stairway to Heaven'. Some of the crowd are as young as three and four years old, and some must be well into their eighties, and yet every single one of them knows every single word to every single one of Rolf's songs. For a complete foreigner, he has become a firmly established part of our English heritage.

He has had a quite amazing career. When I was a kid we grew up watching him draw his extraordinary high-speed giant cartoons. Many years ago we very nearly bought a house in Berkshire, with the River Thames at the bottom of the garden and Rolf Harris as our next-door neighbour. Actually, we only found out who our famous neighbour might have been after the deal had fallen through, and Ingrid, my wife, said, 'That's a great shame really because he'd have been great for decorating!' And I suppose, if we'd wanted a beautiful

Thames-side house with all the walls covered in giant hopping cartoon kangaroos, she was right!

ROGER WHITTAKER

Roger Whittaker, one of the world's most celebrated whistlers, is an old friend of Rolf's, and has been ever since their first encounter nearly forty years ago. The wedding dance song, 'Ye Le', from the movie Zulu, *is a notoriously hard piece of music to execute, but Rolf and Roger decided to perform it when Roger made a guest appearance on* The Rolf Harris Show.

Rolf and I met in the Sixties, when everybody's music was played on *Top of the Pops* and the BBC live programmes. It wasn't broken up and fragmented into as many different genres as it is today. And that was great, because it meant we were able to meet so many different people. There was every kind of artist you could imagine, from pop to folk singers and comedians who played guitars. We would regularly do radio shows with the Beatles, Cilla Black and a wide variety of artists.

I remember going into the BBC Paris Studios in Lower Regent Street, and there was a guy drawing a picture of a bass player hanging over a big double bass. I looked over his shoulder and thought Wow! That's good; he's a talented artist, and it turned out to be Rolf Harris. I told him his drawing impressed me and he, in turn, took a real shine to my whistling. Rolf adores specialist sounds; he loves his wobble-board and didgeridoo and, of course, his Ee-fin' and Eye-fin'. He invited me on to his Saturday evening show to do 'Mexican Whistler', followed by the wedding-dance song from the movie *Zulu* as a joint performance. Rolf was a huge fan of the music from that film, and he came to stay at our house to rehearse it. He brought his didgeridoo, and was still playing it at some ungodly hour. The next day, the neighbours asked what was wrong with our plumbing!

Rolf also brought the music with him; he had all the parts for the song written out in different colours, and they were a hell of a mess. He told me he'd spent about sixteen weeks working it out while he was doing a summer season in Yarmouth. I'm better at reading music now, but in those days I wasn't particularly good. He pulled my leg. 'Oh dear, oh dear,' he said. 'I thought you'd be quicker than that.' And every time I called him or talked to him in between the rehearsal and the show, he'd say, 'You took so long!'

On the day of the show we had several rehearsals with the producer, Stewart Morris, and every time we started we were in the wrong key. I had a guitar in my hand, so I said to Rolf, 'Shall I give you the chord?'

'No, no,' he said. 'I'll pitch the note.'

We never got it right once in rehearsals, and Stewart Morris said, 'You tone-deaf bastards!' as he walked out of the theatre. He was furious with us. I think he thought it was really self-centred to perform such a complex piece.

On the night the show was going out live, so there was quite a tense atmosphere. I went over to Rolf after I'd done 'Mexican Whistler', and there was a line of sweat above his moustache. I could tell he was on edge, but he loved the thrill and the adrenalin surge; he lived for it.

In the event, he pitched the note perfectly and the song was amazing – but it could have been a completely different story!

After that, whenever we met in a restaurant or at a function, he'd break into it. He'd stand up and start it, and I'd join in. Everyone in the restaurant would drop their forks and look at us with eyes wide open. We've actually recorded that song, 'Ye Le', several times since, most recently on a Radio 2 show Rolf did to celebrate National Music Week.

We've been friends ever since. He's one of the closest friends I've got in the business, and his family is close to my family. His wife, Alwen, and daughter, Bindi, are very special people, and are incredibly important to Rolf. He's quite wild, very creative and artistic, and he runs on a different time clock to the rest of the world. I remember him staying with us in the country a few years after we had performed 'Ye Le', and I heard this noise at five o'clock in the morning. I got up and went downstairs, and there he was playing the accordion. I said, 'What are you doing?'

He replied, 'Oh, I just had an idea for something.'

I said, 'I know exactly what you mean, but people are trying to sleep.' His mind is always working. He carries a little notebook around with him, and when he gets an idea he jots it down. He probably gets through a notebook a week.

He sketches in it, too. Rolf is an artist to his fingertips. At the top of our stairs is a portrait he did of me in the Seventies. It's absolutely amazing and he did it in about forty minutes; he says it's one of the best portraits he's ever done. He also did one of my mother and father on an airmail-letter form. It's my father to the life, and since his tragic death in 1989 it has become very special to me. He did it in 1971, when I was in the Far East and couldn't get home. I was due to meet him, but I couldn't make it, so he stayed at my parents' instead and drew this wonderful picture.

Rolf is a very normal lad; he hasn't changed because of his success. If he doesn't like something, he'll say so; and if he doesn't like something you've done, he'll say so. But I understand his sense of humour now. He was pulling my leg over the business of taking a long time to learn the music for 'Ye Le'. When I said to him afterwards, 'I'm sorry

I took so long to learn that,' he replied, 'That's all right; it only took us six months!' I said, 'You miserable bug—' But he burst out laughing before I could finish my sentence.

MATTHEW KELLY

Matthew Kelly has presented ITV's hugely popular Stars in Their Eyes *for several years. He particularly enjoyed it when one of his guests pronounced the immortal line, 'Tonight, Matthew, I am going to be Rolf Harris!'*

There was a man called Colin Grethe who appeared on *Stars in Their Eyes* as Rolf, singing 'Two Little Boys'. Funnily enough, he was very like Rolf in many ways. He was a stress manager by profession, and was one of the coolest people I've ever had on the show. He was also one of the most accurate people we've ever had. I remember asking him, 'How are you stress managing what you're doing, being some-body else?'

He answered, 'I'm slowing time down.' And I thought that was very Rolf, because I think that's what he does. He slows time down so that everybody, including himself, can enjoy every moment of what's going on.

On the occasions I've met Rolf he's always been absolutely charm-ing, very encouraging and very kind. In my formative years I was never really a presenter, I was always an actor. I don't think Rolf ever saw himself as a presenter, either; he was just Rolf. Whenever our paths have crossed he has always been a very nurturing, generous and caring person.

Rolf paved the way for people with beards and curly hair in tele-vision! I'll never forget when I was doing the show *Punchlines*. Lenny Bennett once asked me, 'Why have you got a beard? There are no funny people with beards!' And I was able to say, 'What about Rolf Harris?' That shut him up!

Rolf and I have regularly worked for the same panto company, E&B, but we've never been put in the same show together because we always play similar roles. When I was doing my first pantomimes, they always included a Rolf Harris number, which was normally 'Two Little Boys'. One of the great things about Rolf is that every time you go to a theatre dressing room there is a cartoon somewhere that he's done. Every time you walk in the words follow you: 'Can you tell what it is yet?'

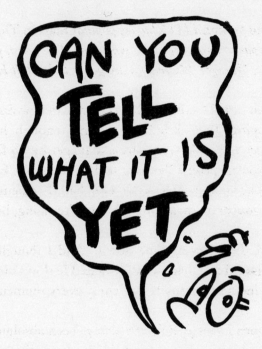

BARBARA WINDSOR

Barbara Windsor appeared with Rolf in the Sixties on The Rolf Harris
Show *with the Young Generation.*

It was switch-on time on a Saturday night with the wonderful *The
Rolf Harris Show*; it was the programme everyone in the business
wanted to be a guest on. Rolf was as huge then as he is now. My family
always watched the programme; Rolf was so funny and the Young
Generation were fantastic. Then one day, out of the blue, I was asked
to appear on the show. I didn't know then, but I was replacing the
comic actress Irene Handl. She had been billed to play the part of a
funny Maid Marian, but as she was unable to make it, they asked me
to take the role. Of course I said yes, I was thrilled to be invited to
appear on such a marvellous programme. But when I got to the studio
they told me I was going to have to sing live! Of course, the show was
going out live, as many programmes did in those days, so I had no
choice, but I was really nervous. When we did the show, Rolf was very
calming and made me feel so at ease, which was terrific. The whole
thing went off really well; it was great fun. Afterwards, as we left the
studio, he said, 'Thank you very much, Barbara, I'm so thrilled you
did that, and I'm so glad we went for a pretty Maid Marian.'

I said, 'What do you mean?' and he replied, 'Well, we were
supposed to have Irene Handl, but she had to pull out because her film
had gone over schedule, so we went for you.'

It was a back-handed compliment, I suppose! But I looked at him
and said, 'Are you kidding?'

Rolf blushed and stammered, 'Oh, I've just realized what I've said.
I'm so sorry.' He gave me a huge hug and we laughed. I remember
running out and getting a really nice bottle of brandy to send it up to
him with a note: 'With my love, and thank you for a wonderful experience. Sorry I'm not Irene Handl!'

Since then we've met occasionally along the way, usually with his
lovely wife, Alwen. They came to see me in a show in the West End,

which was based on the music-hall star Marie Lloyd. He sent me a note saying, 'We're out front in the audience tonight.' Then they came backstage after the show and we went to eat at a little Italian restaurant opposite the theatre. He said, 'I didn't know anything about Marie Lloyd. I only came because you were in the show,' which was very kind and generous.

I was recording an album last year at the same time as I was making *EastEnders*. When I was in the studio someone said, 'Do you know who's in the next studio? It's Rolf Harris!' Apparently he had wanted to come in, but had said, 'Oh, I know Barbara, but I mustn't interfere because she's very busy.' I thought, Blow that, and went running in to say hello, and he played me some of his songs. Rolf can take almost any song and make it his own, like he did with 'Stairway To Heaven'. He's just one of the nicest people I know, and very talented.

STUART MILES

As one of the presenters on Blue Peter, *Stuart Miles enjoyed having Rolf as a guest on the show on more than one occasion.*

There aren't many guests who appear on *Blue Peter* that can be considered legendary figures, but Rolf Harris is definitely one of them. Having watched Rolf when I was young on shows like *Rolf's Cartoon Club*, it was strange as a presenter to welcome him on to *Blue Peter*. In a way, it put my own career and achievements in context, because I thought, I'm interviewing Rolf Harris. Hang on a minute, I used to watch Rolf Harris! I think, for that reason, I felt a little in awe of him.

Rolf has an amazing presence and charisma that comes straight at you when you meet him. Part of the tradition of *Blue Peter* is for the presenters to get involved in the items, and when we had Rolf on to perform 'Sun Arise' it was my role to learn the didgeridoo. As a child I played the clarinet, and although that has very little similarity to the didgeridoo, it at least meant I had some understanding of breath control. Rolf gave me a lesson in rehearsals, but it wasn't just for me, it turned into a routine in front of the studio and crew. They all found it hysterical that I had to have a go on the didgeridoo, so Rolf's lesson became more of a performance, with everyone watching and laughing from the gallery and studio floor, while I was trying my best to learn how to play. I felt more than a little self-conscious blowing into it and making this ridiculous sound. But Rolf has so much enthusiasm for the instrument that it helped me to think, This is fun. Let's just go for it and see if we can make a noise with this thing. In the end I picked it up quite quickly, and had some success at playing it. Maybe the clarinet did help after all!

We had a new dog on the show at that time, called Mabel. She had come from an RSPCA home, and had been through some pretty tough times. She had a problem with men she didn't know, and barked at Rolf when he first came into the studio, but then she got to know him, and started licking his face onscreen. It was very funny; he just bonded with her. It must have been his magic touch with animals coming out. We'd been trying to get the dog to behave for months!

The second time Rolf was a guest on *Blue Peter* he came on to do some artwork. Again, because of the timing of the show and the number of items we have to go through, it all had to be carefully rehearsed. Rolf is one of those professionals who doesn't like to rehearse anything too much, but once he starts there's no stopping him. As he sat there, chatting away while practising his picture, I thought, We could do a whole show with him talking about his drawings. Rolf is the kind of person to whom you could say, 'Here's a camera, here's a piece of paper and here's you. Give us half an hour of live television,' and he would create an interesting programme. He could sit and talk for half an hour and you would be fascinated. I don't think there are many people who could do that. Obviously, for the presenter in a show like *Blue Peter*, it's difficult because you know you have a limited time and that you're going to have to cut Rolf short. It's impossible to know when the right moment is. Rolf's enthusiasm for what he's doing is difficult to stop, and in many ways you don't want to, but unfortunately, in the land of television we have to bring a show out on time, and sometimes you have to subtly tell people to wrap it up. Even, sadly, Rolf Harris!

14

KNIGHTS OF THE ROUND TABLE

Two of Rolf's closest comrades, Sir Harry Secombe and Sir George Martin, are Knights of the Realm and eat regularly at Rolf's table. Both share his love of music and comedy from around the globe, and they have embarked on many crusades together.

SIR HARRY SECOMBE

As a member of the Goons, with their off-the-wall humour and zany characters, Harry Secombe was one of the godfathers of British alternative comedy, as well as being a distinguished and popular singer with a magnificent tenor voice. He has toured the world on numerous occasions, and, as friends, he and Rolf go back forty years.

Rolf was appearing at the Radio Industries Council Exhibition at Earls Court in 1959, and as far as I recall, he was in a sort of booth surrounded by glass, and was taking requests from the visiting kids yelling to him through the glass. He would draw the cartoons they requested on big sheets of card and then pass them out to the kids who'd asked for them. We were doing an interview of some sort that day – the Goons, that is – and were struck by how much the young Rolf resembled Michael Bentine. Rolf's thick, dark curly hair and beard and dark horn-rimmed glasses made him look the image of Mike, who'd only just left the Goons. We gathered round and made great mockery of Rolf, calling him Bentine and cracking all sorts of jokes at his expense. We were expecting him to come back with as good as he got, but the poor fellow was completely bemused and gobsmacked. We eventually had to go and do our interview, and I'm sure he hadn't the faintest idea who we were. That was OK. At that time we didn't know who he was, either. But I soon found out!

One of my earliest memories of time spent with Rolf was in 1961. I remember staying with Rolf and his missus for a weekend in a shack on Palm Beach, north of Sydney. It was a very funny weekend. Rolf heard a noise outside in the night and said, 'That's a koala; there aren't many of them around. Come and take a look.' So we went outside and approached the tree where the koala was residing, and Rolf said, 'I'll go up and talk to it.' He climbed the tree, and the koala, in what I can only assume was an act of self-defence, did a dump on his head! It was hilarious. Rolf had a head full of koala poo and it took a long time to wash out. I sang to him while he was doing it, 'I'm gonna wash that koala poo right outta my hair!'

Rolf has always been a friend and I've known him for many years. The thing with Rolf is that you can pick up exactly where you left off. If you don't see him for five years, you carry on the conversation you were having the last time you saw him.

I think Rolf is a very fine painter. He could paint a ceiling in Rome if he wanted to, and so could Alwen. Their daughter, Bindi, is very good, too; she painted my wife a couple of years ago and it was an excellent portrait. Rolf is also great at photography. I remember years ago walking round Sydney Opera House while it was being built, taking photographs. He hid in a bush and I took photographs of him pretending to be a crook. We were both very impressed with the design of the building.

I used to go out to Australia twice a year for concerts. There were so many places to play over there. You could work in Sydney for about six weeks without playing the same venue twice, which was a blessing in those days! I played at the opera house many times. At the opening we did a show in the concert hall. Cliff Richard closed the first half and I closed the concert. I was bigger in those days. Rolf was there, too. He's such a ubiquitous fellow; he's everywhere. The Queen opened the opera house and we opened the concert hall.

My memories of Rolf are kaleidoscopic. I remember when I had viral pneumonia in Perth, playing in the concert hall there. I was lying on the floor of the dressing room before I went back to the hotel, and he accompanied me, telling me jokes all the way. Then we went to the hospital, and he took me to the maternity department by mistake. He came to visit while I was there; and didn't bring his accordion, thank God! But I wouldn't have been surprised if he had.

He's such a lovely fellow; I'm very fond of Rolf. The last time we were together was down in Cardiff, for the Royal Television Society Awards. We both got enlisted into the Hall of Fame. I think they give you such things for being old these days. As soon as we saw each other we started singing in Welsh. He knows the words to the Welsh National Anthem better than I do.

Rolf's a great fella, a true representative of his country and a great ambassador for Australia. He'll always be a great mate.

SIR GEORGE MARTIN

George Martin was renowned throughout the Sixties for his work as the Beatles' producer. Not so well documented is the fact that he produced many other acts during that era, including, in the early Sixties, all Rolf's hits, such as 'Tie Me Kangaroo Down, Sport', 'Sun Arise', 'The Court of King Caractacus' and 'Six White Boomers'. Since that time Rolf and George have remained close friends.

It seems such a long time ago that I can't recall how I first met Rolf. I was working for EMI at Manchester Square, which has now been pulled down, and I'd heard about what he'd been doing in Australia.

I don't even remember who introduced us, but we started making records together. What I do remember is how impressed I was with Rolf because he was such a multi-talented person. He wasn't just a performer; he was a very good painter, a visual man and a good speaker, as well as being a songwriter and entertainer. He did everything.

One of the early songs we recorded was 'Sun Arise'. When we started on that he had written the basic part, but it went on in the same form and, to be honest, it was a bit boring. I told him what I thought: that it was good, but that it needed something more, and that he needed to write another part for the middle. He tried to persuade me that it was authentic as it was, but he eventually wrote another section, and then it was fine. It was a very good record. His didgeridoo has a unique sound, and so we capitalized on that. Rolf is a great lover of the accordion, too, and he plays it on 'The Court of King Caractacus'. That was one of many songs that came from Rolf's cabaret act; he's got a lot of naughty songs, too!

We always had lots of people in the studio for those recordings. One evening I remember trying to record an album of a live show. Rather inadvisably I invited a lot of expat Australians who happened to be in London to be in the audience. We had got in touch with the Australian embassy to find them. But then, even more inadvisably, I provided them with lots of Fosters, and it became a bit of a nightmare because they all got completely out of hand. In the middle of the recording they were shouting things like, 'Come on, get your arse down here,' and all manner of ribald stuff. We managed to get the recording through, but it was pretty hairy!

At about that time Rolf painted a mural of a bush scene for me, which I stuck up in my office. It covered the complete wall – typical Rolf, slap-dash thing, but it was most effective. It was done on blue paper with black and white highlights. The cover of the first album we recorded together shows him posing in front of it, apparently leaning against one of the trees in the painting. There's a photograph in existence of the Beatles standing in front of it when they came into my office.

Rolf did a New Year's Eve BBC radio show with the Beatles, on which they all sang 'Tie Me Kangaroo Down, Sport' together, though unfortunately I don't think the tapes exist any more. He used his wobble-board for that.

The wobble-board has a great sound, and Rolf is a master of it, always insistent on getting the right intonation. He had several wobble-boards and we used to try different ones. I liked the sound so much I used it on another record that didn't have him on board. I don't know if he knows this, but I took the wobble-board idea and used it as a rhythmic component on a record I made with Peter Sellers and Sophia Loren, which was 'Goodness Gracious Me'. If you listen to it you can hear the sound of a wobble-board.

We became close friends at that time, and Rolf and Alwen came to my wedding. I purposely didn't ask any of the Beatles to the ceremony because I wanted it to be a quiet wedding, not a showbiz affair. Of course, we had one or two personal friends who were showbiz people, like Rolf, Matt Munro and Ron Goodwin, who was our best man, but it was essentially a nice family wedding. We had such a great party afterwards. I was a fellow of London Zoo, so we held our reception in the zoo, with animals all around, which seems rather amusing now that Rolf is a renowned animal-show presenter. Of course, Rolf was the life and soul; he's always performing – never stops! He has a great way of getting things going. If anyone wants their party to go with a swing, invite Rolf Harris; he is the ideal guest.

Rolf is a chameleon; he changes direction, adapts to his backgrounds and metamorphoses all the time. Songs like 'Tie Me Kangaroo Down, Sport' or 'Sun Arise' are completely different from 'Two Little Boys', which I didn't record, though I wish I had. It was a wonderful piece of recording – rather sentimental, but it hit the right spot and was quite distinct from anything he'd done before. He's changed himself once again with *Animal Hospital* and become a serious TV personality, doing something that has struck a chord with many people. It's a compelling show.

A personal thing for me about Rolf is that he turned me on to the beauty of stones. He loves collecting pebbles and unusual bits, and he has a polishing machine at home for them. We have a plate of stones at home which Rolf has collected and polished for us. One of my most treasured possessions is an oil painting he did, *Still Life of Bottles*. It's very good. He just painted it and said, 'Would you like it?'

'Not half, I would!' I quickly replied. So I've got a good painting by Harris, and a good painting by McCartney. But I haven't got a Picasso!

15

THE KING'S SPEECH

ROLF HARRIS

When Mark spoke to me before one of our gigs about his concept for a birthday book, I thought it sounded great. Little did I realize the frantic activity it would plunge him into. As soon as the publishers had approved the idea, with only a six-week deadline, the race was on! His mammoth task included phoning, faxing and e-mailing all around the world to arrange interviews and contributions from over seventy people who in one way or another have played a significant role in my life, and then editing all their information to create this book. He's been amazing, and I take my hat off to him. Now here am I, on 1 January 2000, adding my couple of pence worth.

I would like to thank everyone who has entered into the spirit of this book so wholeheartedly. It has been amazing to find out about so many aspects of my life and the ways I have impinged on other people's lives, many of which I was completely unaware of. There have been so many bits that I just didn't know about, and so many that I'd forgotten. All the things that people had never mentioned, possibly because they thought I wouldn't be interested, have absolutely fascinated me. I must say that I need to take a very strong look at my manners and etiquette regarding driving and being driven. I guess this many people can't be wrong. Perhaps I should invest in some advanced driving lessons.

I would love to say a very special thank you to my immediate family for all the love that shines through the written word. I have found myself close to tears while reading quite a few reminiscences. Finally, to everyone who has involved themselves so open-heartedly in this book, thank you for leaving me with such a warm feeling all over.

lots of love

Rolf

JAKE THE PEG

I'm Jake the Peg, deedle eedle eedle dum
With the extra leg, deedle eedle eedle dum
Wherever I go, through rain and snow
The people always let me know
There's Jake the Peg, deedle eedle eedle dum
With his extra leg, deedle eedle eedle dum

The day that I was born, oh boy my father nearly died
He couldn't get my nappies on, no matter how he tried
'Cause I was born with an extra leg, and since that day begun
I had to learn to stand on my own three feet. Believe me that's not fun.

I'm Jake the Peg . . .

I had a dreadful childhood, well I suppose I shouldn't moan
Each time they had a three-legged race I won it on my own
And also I got popular when came the time for cricket
They used to roll my trousers up and use me for the wickets.

I'm Jake the Peg . . .

I was a dreadful scholar, I found all the lessons hard
The only thing I knew for sure was three feet make a yard
To count to ten I used my fingers, if I needed more
By getting my shoes and socks off I could count to twenty-four.

I'm Jake the Peg . . .

[falters, then counts] . . . one, two, three [etc, up to] twenty-four
[pauses] . . . to twenty-five!

I'm Jake the Peg, deedle eedle eedle dum
With the extra leg, deedle eedle eedle dum
Whatever I did they said was false
They said, 'Quick march!', I did a quick waltz
And then they shouted at me, 'Put your
best foot forward!' 'But which foot?'
I said, 'It's very fine for you, you
Only got a choice of two
But me, I'm Jake the Peg
Deedle eedle eedle dum
With the extra leg, deedle eedle eedle dum . . .'

Two Little Boys
(When We Were Two Little Boys)

Two little boys had two little toys
Each had a wooden horse
Gaily they'd play, each summer's day
Warriors both, of course

One little chap then had a mishap
Broke off his horse's head
Wept for his toy, then cried for joy
As his young playmate said

Did you think I would leave you crying
When there's room on my horse for two
Climb up here, Jack, and don't be crying
I can go just as fast with two

When we grow up we'll both be soldiers
And our horses will not be toys
And I wonder if we'll remember
When we were two little boys

Long years passed, war came so fast
Bravely they marched away
Cannon roared loud, and in the mad crowd
Wounded and dying lay

Up goes a shout, a horse dashes out
Out from the ranks so blue
Gallops away to where Joe lay
Then came a voice he knew

Did you think I would leave you dying
When there's room on my horse for two
Climb up here, Joe, we'll soon be flying
I can go just as fast with two

Did you say, Joe, I'm all a-tremble
Perhaps it's the battle's noise
But I think it's that I remember
When we were two little boys

SUN ARISE

Sun arise she bring in the morning
Sun arise bring in the morning
Fluttering her skirts all around
Sun arise she come with the dawning
Sun arise come with the dawning
Spreading all the light around.

Sun arise on the kangaroo paw
Sun arise on the kangaroo paw
Glistening the dew all around
Sun arise, filling all the hollows
Sun arise, filling all the hollows
Lighting up the hills all around

Sun arise come with the dawning
Sun arise she come every day
Sun arise bring in the morning
Sun arise every every every every day
She drive away the darkness every day
Drive away the darkness
Bringing back the warmth to the ground

Sun arise, oh, oh, sun arise, oh, oh
Spreading all the light all around
Sun arise bring in the morning
Sun arise bring in the morning
Sun arise bring in the morning
Spreading all the light all around

THE COURT OF KING CARACTACUS

Now the ladies of the harem of the court of King Caractacus were just
   passing by
Now the ladies of the harem of the court of King Caractacus were just
   passing by
Now the ladies of the harem of the court of King Caractacus were just
   passing by
Now the ladies of the harem of the court of King Caractacus were just
   passing by

Now the noses on the faces of the ladies of the harem of the court of
   King Caractacus were just passing by
(repeat three times)

Now the boys who put the powder on the noses of the ladies of the
   harem of the court of King Caractacus were just passing by.
(repeat three times)

Now the fascinating witches who put the scintillating stitches in the
britches of the boys who put the powder on the noses of the faces of
the ladies of the harem of the court of Kig Caractacus were just passing by.
(repeat three times)

Now if you want to take some pictures of the fascinating witches who
put the scintillating stitches in the britches of the boys who put the
powder on the noses of the faces of the ladies of the harem of the court
of King Caractacus
You're too late!
Because they've just . . . passed . . . by.

TIE ME KANGAROO DOWN, SPORT

There's an old Australian stockman
Lying
Dying
And he gets himself up onto one elbow
And he turns to his mates, who are gathered round
And he says:

Watch me wallaby's feed, mate,
Watch me wallaby's feed.
They're a dangerous breed, mate,
So watch me wallaby's feed.
All together now!

Tie me kangaroo down, sport,
Tie me kangaroo down.
Tie me kangaroo down, sport,
Tie me kangaroo down.

Keep me cockatoo cool, Curl,
Keep me cockatoo cool.
Don't go acting the fool, Curl,
Just keep me cockatoo cool.
All together now!

(repeat chorus)

Take me koala back, Jack,
Take me koala back.
He lives somewhere out on the track, Mac,
So take me koala back.
All together now!

(repeat chorus)

Mind me platypus duck, Bill
Mind me platypus duck.
Don't let him go running amok, Bill,
Mind me platypus duck.
All together now!

(repeat chorus)

Play your didgeridoo, Blue,
Play your didgeridoo.
Keep playing till I shoot through, Blue,
Play your didgeridoo.
All together now!

(repeat chorus)

Tan me hide when I'm dead, Fred,
Tan me hide when I'm dead.
(*spoken*) So we tanned his hide when he died, Clyde,
And that's it hanging on the shed.
All together now!

(*repeat chorus*)